Town&Country

The

BRIDESMAID'S
COMPANION

CONTENTS

"A happy bridesmaid makes a happy bride."

—Alfred Lord Tennyson

Design by Chika Azuma
Illustrations by Bill Donovan

    Library of Congress Cataloging-in-Publication Data
Town & country the bridesmaid's companion : the complete guide to attending
the bride / Valerie Berrios.
    p. cm.
  Includes index.
  ISBN 978-1-58816-795-8
  1. Wedding etiquette. I. Berrios, Valerie. II. Town & country (New York,
N.Y.) III. Title: Town and country the bridesmaid's companion.
  BJ2051.T69 2009
  395.2'2—dc22
                                    2009030951

10 9 8 7 6 5 4 3 2 1

Published by Hearst Books
A division of Sterling Publishing Co., Inc.
387 Park Avenue South, New York, NY 10016

Town & Country is a registered trademark
of Hearst Communications, Inc.

www.townandcountrymag.com

For information about custom editions, special sales, premium and corporate
purchases, please contact Sterling Special Sales Department at 800-805-5489 or
specialsales@sterlingpublishing.com.

Distributed in Canada by Sterling Publishing
c/o Canadian Manda Group, 165 Dufferin Street
Toronto, Ontario, Canada M6K 3H6

Distributed in Australia by Capricorn Link (Australia) Pty. Ltd.
P.O. Box 704, Windsor, NSW 2756 Australia

Printed in the USA

ISBN 978-1-58816-795-8

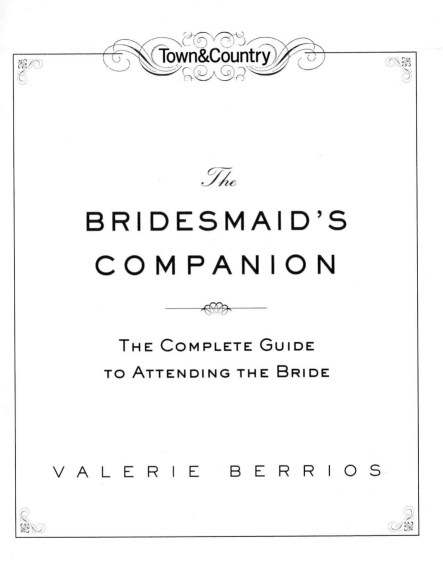

Town&Country

The

BRIDESMAID'S COMPANION

THE COMPLETE GUIDE
TO ATTENDING THE BRIDE

VALERIE BERRIOS

HEARST BOOKS
A division of Sterling Publishing Co., Inc.

New York / London
www.sterlingpublishing.com

FOREWORD

Anyone who has ever been a bridesmaid is aware of the baggage that accompanies that role, from the jokes ("Always a bridesmaid, never a bride") to the fear of winding up in one of those dreadful poufy dresses of yore. Fortunately, most of that is more folklore than fact. Today's attendants are usually stylishly clad and as often married or even pregnant as they may be single. Moreover, they play an important part both prior to and at the actual event.

In its long history of covering weddings—*Town & Country* was founded in 1846—the magazine has paid a great deal of attention to the bride, but not much to the wedding party. We thought it was time for a change for several reasons. Weddings have become bigger productions, and the planning of them can be the equivalent of a full-time job for many a bride-to-be. She needs all the help she can get, and that includes advice and assistance from the members of her wedding party.

Being asked by a bride-to-be to perform the duties of a maid or matron of honor or one of her bridesmaids is both a privilege and an expression of affection and is not to be accepted lightly. It is also an obligation and entails more than merely showing up in a matching dress and leading the way down the aisle. There are real responsibilities to be performed and certain rules of etiquette to be observed. The maid or matron of honor, for example, is also a legal witness at the ceremony. The bridesmaids may be expected to host a shower for the bride-to-be. All of this requires attention, time and, frequently, money.

The Bridesmaid's Companion has been specifically created for these women, who are not only an important presence at the ceremony and the reception, but may well have been assigned tasks leading up to the main event. The bride may also need their emotional support, relying on them to provide honest answers when tough questions arise (as they inevitably will), acting as morale boosters or, if necessary, smoothers of ruffled feathers.

Think of it this way: if the wedding is a feature film and the bride and groom are its stars, then the wedding party is akin to the supporting cast. Without them, the stars won't shine nearly as brightly.

Pamela Fiori

Editor in Chief, *Town & Country*

Being asked to be a bridesmaid isn't something you should ever take for granted. Just think: out of everyone the bride has ever known, she chose you (and only a handful of others) to stand with her on one of the biggest, most emotional, truly unforgettable days of her life. It's a touching moment, a great honor, and undeniably a huge responsibility.

Whether this is your first time in the position or your fifth time up to bat, *The Bridesmaid's Companion* will help you navigate all the dos and don'ts of this sometimes-demanding yet highly rewarding role. So, yes, there will be stressful times and the unavoidable ups and downs that come with planning a wedding. The bride will be counting on you to help her get through many of them—whether you're offering advice (should she go with ankle-length or floor-length bridesmaids' gowns?), tracking down that missing veil, or simply listening to her vent about her attention-craving mother-in-law. This book guides you as you handle these issues and many more—from party planning (timelines included) and dress shopping (learn how to flatter all shapes and sizes, including the pregnant bridesmaid) to your big-day duties and beyond (you want to be friends for life, right?).

The good news is there will be plenty of moments that make all the effort worthwhile. Planning a fabulously girly bridal shower, living it up during a bachelorette-party weekend getaway, seeing your friend transformed from single to coupled right before your eyes, silly bridesmaids' dances you'll laugh about for years—it's all part of being a bridesmaid. Take a look at the stories and quotes from brides and bridesmaids past sprinkled throughout this book, and you'll be reminded why you signed on.

Never been a bridesmaid? Or hoping to be a better one this time around? *The Bridesmaid's Companion* will help you sort out everything from e-mail protocol to terrific toasts to making a keepsake the bride will cherish. If you're single (but expecting Mr. Right to pop the question one of these days), you'll inevitably think of your own wedding as you read this book, and that's a good thing. The moral of the story is that bridesmaids should do their best to support the bride before, during, and after the wedding; in return, the bride should always treat her bridesmaids with respect and appreciation, no matter what bridal stresses are coming her way. And, with this code of conduct in place, you will joyfully return the favor when it's your turn to walk down the aisle.

BRIDESMAIDS: THEN AND NOW

Congratulations! You are about to become part of a tradition that's as old as it is revered. The history of bridesmaids dates back to the Roman era, when the bride would travel to the groom's town or village accompanied by a group of similarly dressed women, a ruse to help guard her from robbers, bandits, and kidnappers. Other historians trace the origin of bridesmaids to biblical times. In the Book of Genesis, Jacob's two wives, Leah and Rachel, are escorted to their wedding by handmaidens. The Romans eventually made it law for a marrying couple to have ten witnesses present at their wedding to protect them from misfortune brought on by evil spirits. The attendants were required to wear the same attire as the bride and groom in order to confuse the spirits who wished to bring harm to the newlyweds.

The tradition of the couple and their attendants dressing alike continued well into the nineteenth century, as many people still believed that a couple could be cursed by ill-wishers on their wedding day. In later years, the number of attendants in a wedding party signified the family's status in the community. In essence, the more attendants you had, the wealthier you were. Today things aren't so gloomy—or materialistic. Now it's perfectly acceptable for a bride to have just one bridesmaid or two female attendants, especially if the wedding is an intimate affair.

So what exactly is a bridesmaid? She's typically a young woman who is a close friend, sister, or cousin of the bride. The bride's best friend or closest relative is often picked to be the principal bridesmaid and receives the title of "maid of honor," also known as "chief bridesmaid" or "honor attendant." When the woman taking on this role is married, she's called the "matron of honor." Girls who are too young to be bridesmaids yet too old to be flower girls (ages nine to fourteen) may receive the honorary title of "junior bridesmaids." They often wear dresses similar to the bridesmaids' gowns, but they are, of course, age appropriate (i.e., no strapless or low-cut styles). You'll learn more about their duties in Chapter 1, page 36.

A FEW WORDS ON ETIQUETTE

There's no doubt that times have changed. Since texting "I love you," instant-messaging your boss, and sending virtual gifts via Facebook applications have become the norm, etiquette rules on traditional forms of communication have taken a back seat. Sending someone a handwritten invitation instead of an Evite is archaic, right? Wrong. At least, thankfully, when it comes to weddings.

Many bridal traditions, including the specific roles of wedding attendants, remain alive and well. For example, it's still not acceptable to e-mail an invitation to a bridal shower; if you have ecological concerns, there are plenty of stationery companies that sell beautiful card stocks made with recycled paper or natural fibers like cotton and hemp, or invitations embedded with plantable wildflower seeds.

Of course it's appropriate to incorporate modern touches (yes, the bridesmaids *can* wear black), but there's something so pure—and just plain romantic—about sticking to rituals that generations before you have followed.

For you, as the bridesmaid, knowing the established rules will help you determine your role, remove any doubts you may have about your obligations, and make planning prewedding events that much easier. Etiquette guidelines will also clue you in on how to present yourself during the ceremony and reception. Needless to say, the bride is counting on you to be on your best behavior—remember, you're standing with her on one of the most precious days of her life, as one of the closest people in her circle. Now's not the time to give an off-color speech about her wild college years, get embarrassingly drunk at the rehearsal dinner, or publicly make out with a guest during the reception. In short: set an example!

Cʜ. *1*

WHAT'S EXPECTED OF YOU

As a bridesmaid, you have numerable responsibilities. Some may seem like a burden—such as forking over upward of two hundred dollars for a gown you may never wear again or coordinating a bridal shower when all seven bridesmaids live in different states. But others are no more than you'd do anyway for the friend who stood by you during those awkward teen years or through the drama of dating a slew of Mr. Wrongs.

Some duties simply require you to show up. Aside from the obvious events (the rehearsal, ceremony, and reception) and the celebrations you're cohosting (the shower and bachelorette party), the only events you *must* attend are the rehearsal dinner, typically held the night before the wedding, and the postwedding brunch, if there is one. Any other wedding festivities on the schedule, such as family-hosted engagement parties, are optional. However, you should try to attend as many of them as you can—it's a good show of support. And besides, who doesn't love a party?

Getting invited to a few VIP events is part of the excitement of being a bridesmaid. It's also important to remember that in addition to your physical contributions, the bride will need you to stand by her emotionally throughout this process. If she's clashing with her mom about the bridesmaids' bouquets or cake design, let her know that you support her long-held dream of a fuchsia calla lily arrangement or an Art Deco cake. And if she's the type who feels uncomfortable asking for help—even when she desperately needs it—be the one to step up and offer to call the florist or pick up the wedding gown. Helping with the little things is what being the bride's attendant is all about.

YOUR JOB IN A NUTSHELL

You already know that you're required to attend the ceremony and reception, but here's a rundown of your other major responsibilities. See page 138 for a timeline of tasks leading up to the main event.

- Provide practical and emotional support and creative input.

- Help shop for bridesmaid dresses and pay for your entire ensemble.

- Assist with prewedding tasks, such as scheduling dress fittings and affixing personalized labels onto guest favors.

- Formally RSVP to the wedding by the requested date—this is especially important if you plan to bring a guest.

- Help organize, cohost, and pay for the bridal shower and bachelorette party.

- Choose a bridal shower gift for the bride and a wedding gift for the couple.

- Attend the ceremony rehearsal, rehearsal dinner, postwedding brunch, and as many other scheduled events as possible.

- Keep copies of any readings that people will be reciting during the ceremony.

- Assist the bride with wedding-day errands, such as confirming that all deliveries (cakes, flowers, etc.) have been made.

- Be on time for wedding photographs.

- Greet guests in the receiving line, at the bride's request.

- Encourage guests to get on the dance floor.

- Enjoy being a VIP guest and have a fabulous time!

MONEY MATTERS

Taking on the role of a bridesmaid is a huge time commitment with financial obligations. You probably already know that you're responsible for paying for your own gown, but you should also know that you're expected to pay for the alterations and provide or buy your shoes, jewelry, and other accessories. Do you live in another state? Or will it be a destination wedding? If so, add travel expenses and hotel accommodations to your budget. Most brides will help offset costs by securing rooms at one or two nearby hotels at a discounted rate. Some airlines also offer group rates, so be sure to check into that option. The bride may be able to help coordinate these arrangements.

You will also be asked to chip in for expenses related to the bridal shower and bachelorette party. If a bachelorette weekend getaway is in the works, the bill for the entire trip should be split evenly among the bridesmaids. As for gifts, you'll be expected to give one at the bridal shower in addition to the wedding gift. For the former, consider pooling your money with the rest of the bridesmaids to purchase one big-ticket item. It may also take the pressure off to know that the latter can be given up to a year after the wedding—but these days, when all you have to do is go online, point, click, and ship a prewrapped gift, there's no excuse for such a long delay. It's best to send your wedding gift within two months.

HER GO-TO GIRLS

Planning a wedding can be downright daunting—you've seen *Father of the Bride*—so amid all the appointment booking, decision-making, and other chaos, the bride needs you. Even with her mother in the wings, she can't do it all. You'll be there to keep her steady (physically and emotionally) both before the wedding and on the big day.

❧

••• FAR AND AWAY •••

The good news: you're asked to be a bridesmaid, and the wedding's in Cabo San Lucas. The bad news: the wedding's in Cabo San Lucas. That means you're responsible for the expenses that go along with a destination wedding—travel, lodging, gratuities . . . you get the picture.

If you needed a vacation anyway, fantastic. Make the most of it. But if this wedding trip will put a crimp in your budget, either think twice before accepting the invitation to be a bridesmaid or simply know what to expect. The bride will give you advance notice, so you'll have plenty time to save up for it—even if that means cutting back on a few luxuries. On the plus side, you will probably receive a group rate for your flight and/or hotel.

Another good thing about destination weddings is that your duties may be reduced, as most of the details are typically arranged by the on-site planner. Nonetheless, you should still be ready and willing to help the bride with any to-dos, like putting together personalized welcome baskets for guests filled with local treats, city maps, and travel brochures. Expect to be invited to a welcome dinner in addition to the rehearsal dinner and at least one postwedding celebration.

*"At her engagement party,
a close friend of mine invited me
and several other female friends into
a private room and had envelopes
waiting for us with personalized
notes asking each of us to be
in her wedding party.
I was extremely excited and honored
that she asked me to be a part
of her wedding."* —Jessica

The Planning Stages

The days leading up to the ceremony and reception will offer plenty of opportunities to fulfill your duties. You may be asked to take on some or all of the following tasks.

HELP PREP INVITATIONS OR FAVORS. If called upon, be ready to do some busy work, such as stuffing and sealing envelopes or tying ribbons or tags onto favor boxes. To help make these tasks less of a chore, download a playlist of cheesy pop music to blast from an iPod dock, uncork a bottle of wine, and take advantage of the chance to bond with your fellow bridesmaids.

HELP SHOP FOR DRESSES AND ACCESSORIES. The maid of honor is typically assigned this role, but the bride may also ask another bridesmaid or two to tag along on shopping jaunts for a second or third opinion. Make a day of it and have a quiet sit-down lunch in between boutique stops.

ATTEND FORMAL DRESS FITTINGS. A super-organized bride might want to make sure all her maids are fitted at the same time, so she'll book the appointments herself. Otherwise, you'll be expected to schedule your own fittings (ideally, two) before the wedding.

ANSWER QUESTIONS ABOUT THE WEDDING. For example, guests who are closer to you than to the parents of the bride or groom may turn to you for registry information or to find out if childcare will be provided for the adults-only wedding. So be sure you're in the know.

Today's the Day

Here's the fun part. The day has finally arrived. The bride may have some butterflies but she's undoubtedly excited to tie the knot and begin her new life. Thanks to the rehearsal the day before, you'll have the processional and recessional down pat, you'll know who's escorting you down the aisle, and you'll know exactly where to stand at the altar. Perfect. But, as her bridesmaid, you've still got lots to do.

HELP THE BRIDE GET READY. This may be your final chance to bond with the bride before she becomes a Mrs., so make it memorable by popping open a bottle of bubbly and toasting to her happiness. While the bride's getting ready, the maid of honor or another bridesmaid should make sure there are bottles of water available and plenty of healthy snacks for her and the rest of the crew to munch on—finding time to eat a proper meal can be tough amid

••• The Fabulous at Forty (Plus) Bride •••

If the bride is over forty, chances are you and the rest of the bridesmaids are in the same age range. Attending to an older bride involves virtually the same responsibilities as attending to a bride in her twenties or thirties; a key difference is that an older bride often chooses sophistication over frilliness (i.e., no poufy princess gowns for her). It could also be the bride's second or third marriage, so she might opt for something more intimate or low-key this time around. The shower should also reflect a more mature vibe, so skip the pastel table linens and perhaps the Bridal Bingo.

An older bride and groom are also likely to be in a better financial position than a younger couple would be, so they might be footing the bill for all or most of the wedding—thus reducing the potential for family conflicts and overall stress. That may mean less work for you, but you should still offer to assist in any way you can. The key is to be specific about what you'd like to help with. For example, does she need you to send an e-mail to the other bridesmaids about her gown picks or recommend hotels for the out-of-town guests? Offer services that you can perform reliably and make it clear that you are happy to assist.

all the prewedding hoopla. Remember that practically every moment of the bride's preparation—from hair and makeup application to the momentous zipping or buttoning of the gown—will be captured by a professional photographer, videographer, and/or a beaming mother of the bride, so keep things PG.

KEEP COPIES OF CEREMONY READINGS. One of the bridesmaids should have a backup copy of each ceremony reading, just in case a reader forgets to bring the scripture, poem, or passage he or she intends to recite.

RUN ANY LAST-MINUTE ERRANDS, AS REQUESTED BY THE BRIDE. Wedding planners are typically on hand to confirm cake and flower delivery times or set out the wedding programs. But if the bride doesn't have a planner or needs additional assistance, that's when you come in.

ASSIST WITH ANY EMERGENCIES. With all the many months of planning that typically go into a wedding, you'd think nothing could possibly go wrong. Unfortunately, that's wishful thinking. The easiest way to deal with minor issues, such as a ripped hem or a lipstick stain on the bride's gown, is to have an emergency kit at the ready. Simply fill a case or tote bag with a few essentials. Use the list below to get started.

- Band-Aids
- Pain relievers
- Facial tissues
- Corsage pins
- Straight pins
- Mini sewing kit
- Folding scissors
- Tweezers
- Dental floss
- Breath mints
- Stain remover
- Clear nail polish (for stocking runs)
- Hairspray
- Tampons/sanitary napkins

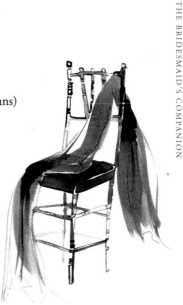

My bridesmaids created a beautiful scrapbook for me before the wedding. They had gathered photographs and letters from all the early parts of my life—including a spread from my dad, childhood friends and their parents, my first boyfriend, and of course my husband.

—Jenny

For the big emergencies—like the limo getting stuck in standstill traffic, an MIA photographer, an ice sculpture with the wrong monogram on it, a chuppah blowing over before the ceremony starts, or sparklers setting off a small fire—the first thing to do is reassure the bride that these things happen. Then work as a team to remedy the situation as quickly—and discreetly—as possible. In the case of a no-show vendor, call the office and have them send over a replacement ASAP. Other unexpected problems like traffic or an incorrect monogram just have to be taken in stride.

SERVE AS COHOSTESS AT THE RECEPTION. As part of the wedding party, you're considered an honorary hostess. So take the time to introduce yourself to guests and them to one another. Help early arrivers find their seats, direct guests to the bar, and invite everyone to sign the guest book.

STAND IN THE RECEIVING LINE. The bridal party is often invited to take part in the receiving line at the start of the reception. It's a chance for guests to personally congratulate the newlyweds and for the couple to thank the guests for their attendance. Because it's important to keep the line of well-wishers moving (and get on with the festivities), bridesmaids should keep chats with guests short and sweet.

BE AVAILABLE FOR PHOTOGRAPHS. When it's time to snap the group portraits (either before the wedding or following the ceremony), it's essential that you're on time and ready to go when the photographer is. Wedding-day photos don't have to be stressful as long as everyone sticks to the schedule.

ENCOURAGE THE GUESTS TO HAVE FUN. After the traditional first dances, when the band starts jamming or the DJ begins his playlist, guests are free to hit the dance floor. Because many people feel uncomfortable being the first ones in the spotlight, it's usually the bridesmaids who get the party started by dancing to a song selected just for them. If there's no official bridesmaids' dance, every maid should get up anyway, grab a groomsman (or not), and shake her groove thing. Spot a toe-tapping guest without an escort? Offer to be his dance partner.

IT'S PARTY TIME!

Another fun part of being a bridesmaid is helping to plan and cohost the bridal shower and bachelorette party. It may require a fair amount of time and careful coordination—

but with the right leader at the helm (the faithful maid of honor) it should be no trouble at all.

Shower Her with Love

The maid of honor is technically the hostess, but she will no doubt enlist the other maids to help with costs (split evenly) and logistics. Although coed showers are gaining popularity (see Boys Allowed, page 81), this event is often still dedicated to the bride and attended by a few of her closest female friends and relatives ready to shower her with gifts. Depending on how many people are coming from out of town, it can be held anywhere from six months to one week before the wedding. The party is traditionally a lunch or an intimate gathering at someone's home, but if the bride is a backyard barbecue type, then anything goes. It's common to have themed showers, such as a lingerie, white linen, cooking, or dessert party. You'll read more about themed parties in Chapter 4, page 80.

Let Your Hair Down!

After the shower comes the bachelorette party—a casual, fun-filled girls' night out (perhaps at a lounge or comedy club) or a girls' night in (think "poker night"). It's typically held at the same time as the groom's bachelor party, from a month to a week before the wedding. The invitation list is significantly shorter than for the shower, and the invites can be as informal as an Evite or a phone call. The cost of the party is divided among all of the guests. Mothers of the bride and groom and older relatives are usually left off the guest list—unless the bride is comfortable letting loose in front of her elders. Just remember to respect the bride's comfort level. If checking out a male revue is not her thing, don't go there. In Chapter 4, page 91, we provide tips on planning a bachelorette bash the bride won't soon forget.

OTHER THOUGHTFUL GESTURES

Being a bridesmaid means taking time, money, and effort to help your friend or relative prepare for one of the biggest events of her life. These things will be appreciated, but if the bride has been extra generous and equally supportive of you, why not consider some other gestures that are certainly not required but nice just the same? For example, if either family needs help with the logistics of planning the engagement party or the rehearsal dinner because they live elsewhere, and you're already familiar with the area, lend a hand by offering venue suggestions. Helping with odds and ends like these shouldn't take much more of your time—but if it does, don't overextend yourself.

A NOTE OF THANKS. You've been invited to be a bridesmaid, and you've happily accepted. Terrific! If the bride is a dear friend or a close relative, now is the perfect opportunity to send her an old-fashioned thank you note. Go to your favorite stationery shop and pick out a card that has just the right message or purchase a beautiful blank card so you can express in your own words how much being a part of her wedding party means to you.

PERSONAL KEEPSAKES. The bride will want to remember every second of her wedding as well as all the happy events leading up to it, but she may not have the time to think about anything past the upcoming wedding. So while she's planning away, team up with the other bridesmaids to collect dress swatches, sample invitations, programs, menu cards, and so on. Then combine these mementos with the group's favorite candid shots from the past few months to create a nice little scrapbook you all can present to her after she comes down from her wedding high. For a sweet bridal shower keepsake, fill a guest book with a photo of each attendee and invite everyone to write a special message next to her picture. Or ask each guest to design a scrapbook page for the bride and bring it to the shower. One of the bridesmaids can collect all the pages and put the book together for the guest of honor.

FOR THE HAPPY COUPLE. Once the wedding's over, the honeymoon is a welcome relief for the couple. All the stresses they endured as they planned their wedding (the expenses, the family drama, the tiffs about whether they really needed to register for china) can be set aside for a week or two to just relax and unwind. To help make their trip extra special, the bridesmaids can collectively arrange to have a basket of goodies (such as champagne, fresh fruit, and chocolate truffles) delivered to the couple's honeymoon suite to welcome them to marital bliss.

JUNIOR BRIDESMAIDS

If the bride has junior bridesmaids in the wedding, you may wonder what their roles entail. Well, since they're children (typically ages nine to fourteen), their duties are of course limited. But because a junior bridesmaid is part of the wedding party, it's a nice gesture to make her feel

··· CHILD'S PLAY ···

When children are part of the wedding party—as they often are—it adds a charming innocence to the ceremony. Who can forget the adorable flower girl who pranced down the aisle scattering rose petals from her basket as though the event were all about her? Or the four-year-old ring bearer who decided it was more fun to carry his cushion on top of his head?

Before the wedding, bridesmaids may not have a lot of contact with the flower girl, ring bearer, or other child attendants. It's only during the rehearsal that everyone finally comes together—and this time can be the most critical in ensuring the kids are comfortable in their roles and being around the other attendants. A flower girl who's too scared to join the processional or a ring bearer who wails for his parents midway down the aisle is not so cute.

So during the ceremony run-through, try to develop a bond with the children. If they're super-shy or not used to being without their parents at their sides, help reassure them. Think of yourself as the big sister for the day. If a child freezes during any part of the ceremony, take her by the hand and guide her the rest of the way. This will help ensure that the ceremony goes as smoothly as possible.

included. Ask if she'd like to help with small wedding tasks, such as distributing the send-off confetti to guests, or some aspects of planning the bridal shower, which she (and her mother or guardian) would be invited to attend.

The parents of juniors are expected to pay for their wedding attire. Her dress will likely be a more youthful version of the bridesmaids' gowns. She will also attend the bridesmaids' luncheon, the rehearsal, and possibly the rehearsal dinner; walk in the processional; and stand beside the other bridesmaids at the altar. It should go without saying that she would not be invited to a bachelorette party that involves adult activities. And she wouldn't normally be asked to stand in the receiving line.

CH. *2*

THE MAID OF HONOR'S ROLE

She's likely the bride's best friend or sister.
She's the one the bride trusts to help her find her dream gown. She's the lead planner for the bridal shower and bachelorette party. She's the chief bridesmaid—the maid of honor (or matron of honor if she's married). She has a special role, so to help her stand out, the maid of honor often wears a gown that's subtly different from her fellow bridesmaids (either in color or style), wears different jewelry, or holds a unique bouquet (maybe more elaborate than the others or monochromatic instead of multicolored). Her duties are the same as the rest of the bridesmaids, with a few extras thrown in.

If you've been named the honor attendant, consider it a privilege and be prepared to take on the following responsibilities.

KEEP A RECORD OF GIFTS RECEIVED. The bride will receive an overwhelming number of gifts at the bridal shower and other parties, so she'll rely on you to help keep track of who gave what. She'll use the list to send thank-you notes, so it's important to be as specific as possible. Include notes on her reactions if they're particularly memorable.

HANDLE THE GROOM'S WEDDING RING. No, the ring bearer isn't really responsible for this task (imagine!). The best man is in charge of safekeeping the bride's ring during the ceremony, and you're responsible for the groom's band. It's best to wear the ring on your thumb or place it in a small jewelry pouch you can hold in one hand.

HOLD THE BRIDE'S BOUQUET DURING THE VOW EXCHANGE. When the officiant signals that it's time for the couple to exchange vows, the couple will often take one another's hands. At this point, the bride will give you her wedding bouquet to hold until she and the groom are pronounced husband and wife.

ADJUST THE BRIDE'S TRAIN. The bride will need you to help arrange her train, assuming she has one, prior to the processional, after she reaches the altar, and again during the recessional. Work quickly when doing this—you don't want to call too much attention to yourself. Your dress duties don't end there: you'll also need to bustle her gown

"I'm getting married next spring and I've asked my sister to be my maid of honor. She has been my rock, especially after our mom passed away five years ago. My sister actually moved to New York City to help with my wedding planning. I couldn't have asked for a better wedding gift, maid of honor, or sister." —Christina

for the reception. If necessary, enlist a couple of brides-maids to help with this part—it can be tricky. Also be prepared to help the bride when she takes restroom breaks (bridesmaids can take turns with this one).

SERVE AS LEGAL WITNESS OF THE MARRIAGE. The maid of honor and the best man will be requested to sign the marriage certificate or ketubah (the Jewish marriage contract) as witnesses, either during or immediately fol-lowing the ceremony. (Note that you must be Jewish to sign a ketubah.)

OFFER A TOAST AT THE REHEARSAL DINNER AND/OR RECEPTION. Giving a speech at the rehearsal dinner and/or reception is optional, but it can be a meaningful gesture. At the reception, you can give your toast after the best man (the official toastmaster) gives his. For tips on toasting, see page 134.

HELP THE BRIDE CHANGE INTO HER GOING-AWAY ATTIRE. If the couple is leaving for the honeymoon im-mediately after their grand exit, the bride will often change into a more comfortable ensemble, such as a simple white dress with a higher hemline. You can make this switch seamless by accompanying her to the dressing room and helping her get ready. You can also make sure the couple's luggage is ready for their departure.

THE BRIDE'S RIGHT HAND

First and foremost, your role as maid or matron of honor is to be there for the bride every step of the way. Helping her shop for her gown, organize the guest list and seating chart, safeguard the rings—all these things are important. But the most memorable way you can fulfill your role is by providing good-old emotional support. Planning a wedding is demanding for the bride, so she'll need a confidante to vent her frustrations to, get reassurances from, or simply gab with to take her mind off the wedding for a while.

Help Her Stress Less

The bride will likely find herself in more than one sticky situation on the road to the altar—whether it's the disastrous dye job she receives the day before the wedding or last night's petty argument with the groom that has her threatening to call the whole thing off. Sometimes the most effective way to diffuse her prewedding stress is to encourage her to schedule some "me" time. You can bring her back to the blissful place she was in when her guy popped the question by offering the following tips.

DO WEDDING DETOX. Tell her to take a full twenty-four hours (forty-eight is even better) to not do a single thing related to the wedding. She can dive into a novel she's been meaning to read, schedule a movie marathon with her man, or indulge in some retail therapy.

GET HER MOVING. Exercise will do more than get her body ready for that slinky gown. Going for a jog or taking a long bike ride will help clear her mind, improve her mood, boost her energy, and give her a better night's sleep.

A LITTLE SELF-INDULGENCE. Suggest that she book an hour at the spa for a relaxing massage, facial, or mani-pedi. Or she can stay in and turn her bathroom into a sanctuary by lighting aromatherapy candles and taking a steaming bubble bath.

"On the night before my wedding, I was sick as a dog with jitters. I was also super-stressed since I still had to create all the bouquets and boutonnières. Finally, my matron of honor woke up and had a solution to my worries. She blasted the Commodores's 'Brick House' on the stereo, and we danced in the kitchen until my nerves were calmed."
—Bethany

HEAR THE MUSIC. Lying down, with eyes closed, while she listens to classical or meditative music is a great way for her to reach wedding Zen.

HAVE A LAUGH. Who hasn't experienced the stress-relieving benefits of a good-old laugh-out-loud session? Suggest seeing a funny film, take her to a comedy show, or plan a girls' gabfest where you divulge your most embarrassing tales.

Help Her Resolve Conflicts

Certainly, weddings can be rife with drama. And these tense times can put everyone on edge in concentric circles, from the bride and groom to their parents to the wedding party. Before things blow over, the maid of honor should take on the role of chief diplomat and help to defuse these situations. It's most important to remain as objective as possible so no one's feelings get hurt.

When the bride and her mother are waging a war of words, calmly suggest that they figure out a way to compromise. If the mother of the bride is insisting that her daughter go with traditional white invitations, the bride should consider relenting as long as Mom agrees not to give her grief about her decision to go without a veil.

If the issue involves the in-laws, then things can get a bit more complicated. Perhaps the groom's mom graciously offered her wedding ring to his wife-to-be, but the bride already had her heart set on a less ornate style. Or maybe the groom's parents chose a rehearsal dinner venue that was inconvenient for most people on the bride's side of the family. The bride and groom should first have a heart-to-heart to make sure they're on the same page, and then the groom should be the one to explain their concerns with his parents.

LEADER OF THE PACK

One of your primary duties as chief bridesmaid is to manage the other bridesmaids. And with this responsibility comes potential challenges—especially if you're not used to being an Alpha female. The following tips will guide you in this leadership role.

From a Distance

It may seem daunting to coordinate duties with bridesmaids who live out of town. But it doesn't have to be difficult, as long as you keep the following guidelines in mind.

••• E-MAIL ETIQUETTE •••

Using e-mail to send wedding or bridal shower invitations is too informal and impersonal, but it's a great way for bridesmaids to stay up-to-date on the bride's wedding plans and to communicate with one another. Be sure to swap e-mail addresses so you can keep in touch throughout the planning process, and feel free to use them to . . .

- Share pictures and get feedback on bridesmaids' gowns, group gifts, and party venues.
- Coordinate dress fittings.
- Discuss the logistics of the shower and bachelorette party.
- Send invitations to informal events like the bachelorette party.
- Allow guests to RSVP to prewedding events.
- Get to know your fellow bridesmaids—you might discover another lifelong friend.

But don't send an e-mail to . . .
- RSVP for the wedding (use the response card).
- Invite people to the bridal shower.
- Send negative comments about the wedding or anyone in the bridal party (you run the risk of the message accidentally landing in the inbox of the person being bashed).

"We've all grown a lot closer since my wedding, and although none of these women knew one another before my wedding, they have all kept in touch and are forming their own bonds. When I look at images now from my big day, I know that in thirty years I will still be close with each of them, regardless of where we've traveled in our lives."

—Lisa

- Start planning the major tasks and events, like the bridal shower, as soon as possible.

- Use e-mail to keep bridesmaids up-to-date on party plans, dress fittings, and their wedding-day duties.

- Prepare a checklist for the attendants so each one knows her responsibilities.

- Make sure the ladies know their financial obligations; even if a bridesmaid is not attending the shower, she will need to contribute money.

- Get help from family members and other friends of the bride who live near the wedding location.

Can't We All Just Get Along?

Personality clashes between bridesmaids can result in bridal wars. People in the wedding party certainly don't have to be best friends with one another, but if a couple of the attendants aren't getting along it can put a strain on the rest of the bunch—especially when you all team up to plan the shower or bachelorette party.

If there's a bridal-party squabble, as maid of honor you should sit down with each woman individually to hear both sides. If the conflict is more than a simple compromise can fix, then do your best to convince them to play nice at least until after the wedding—for the bride's sake.

BOY AND GIRL WONDER

As the honor attendants, you and the best man have lots in common. As such, you should make sure you're on the same page when it comes to any overlapping duties. For example, the bachelorette and bachelor parties are typically held on the same night or weekend. Because you're in charge of the girls' night and he's the organizer for the boys' night, you'll need to touch base regularly and agree upon a date that works for everyone.

Preparing toasts for the reception is another duty you'll share. In the past, it was only the best man who served as toastmaster, but these days the maid of honor

··· A Gender Bender ···

More likely than not, the bride's honor attendant will be a woman, but modern brides may throw caution to the wind and designate their best male friend as their "man" of honor. Remember Patrick Dempsey's character in *Made of Honor?* Hey, if he's game and your groom doesn't mind, there's absolutely no reason not to do it.

Amy chose a male honor attendant when she got married years ago, in part because she was an avid feminist who ignored traditional gender roles. Looking back, she has no regrets. "It was fun, it made people look twice . . . and to me, it was just like having any friend stand up for me," she says.

At Amy's wedding, the man of honor wore the same tux as the groomsmen but stood at her side during the ceremony. Another way to make him stand out is to give him a different boutonnière that still matches the color of the bridesmaids' dresses. Because it's all about gender equality, male honor attendants are required to fulfill the duties of any other chief bridesmaid. If he needs direction, his female counterparts can be the ones to help clue him in.

has also joined in the fun. Put your heads together to figure out who goes first. If you favor recent tradition, let him warm up the crowd for you. Or, if you have a great rapport with the best man, consider a joint speech—this will require a few practice runs. (For more tips on toasting, see page 134.) Establishing camaraderie with your cohort may come in handy when you're seeking mutual advice about how to rein in the crew or plan the perfect bash.

CH. *3*

THE DRESSES

Sure, you've heard the jokes. "Oh, so you're going to be a bridesmaid? Bet you can't wait to wear the dress." (Cue smirk.) Even recent films like *27 Dresses* poke fun at the long-held belief that these gowns are meant to be worn once and then hidden away in the back of your closet, never to be seen again. That film features a memorable scene in which Katherine Heigl's always-a-bridesmaid character parades around in a bevy of her less-than-flattering ensembles from weddings past.

But relax! You're not doomed to wear something resembling the garish hot pink, puffy-sleeved, shapeless gowns you remember from your great aunt's wedding album. These days, there are tons of beautiful bridesmaids' dresses available, including collections from such top designers as Vera Wang, Badgley Mischka, and Nicole Miller, which will no doubt ensure that you and your fellow attendants are the best-dressed guests at the wedding. Plus, you'll have no qualms about donning one of these beauties for another special occasion or two.

SHOP AROUND

While it's ultimately the bride's decision as to which gown you'll wear (remember, it's her wedding), she'll likely want the maid of honor's input. Therefore, as she narrows down her options, you—and perhaps one or two other bridesmaids—may be asked to accompany her to bridal salons or designer showrooms to check out some dresses. The bride may also send the occasional e-mail with images of dresses she's considering, which would be an excellent opportunity for you to provide some honest feedback.

Keep in mind: she really does want you to look and feel beautiful in your dress, so don't be shy about gently steering her in the right direction—and away from that taffeta number with the oversized bow in front. She might even leave the big decisions up to you. But if she's already set on the exact style and color she wants you and the other ladies to wear, she may simply provide the designer name and style number so that you can order the gown online or purchase it from your local bridal boutique. Once her mind is made up, it's your job to graciously consent to her selection.

"My bridesmaids thought the dresses I picked made them look fat, and they kept joking about being a 'convoy' [a lineup of huge trucks]. So as they went down the aisle they subtly made the gesture you make to a trucker to get him to blow the horn. It was actually pretty funny!"

—Leslie

Styles That Flatter

If the bride solicits your advice while she's gown shopping, make sure she's aware that certain dress styles are universally flattering. For example, an A-line gown creates a smoother, sleeker silhouette that works wonders for everyone, particularly pear-shaped women. Moreover, if the bride is looking for a dress you can wear after the wedding (and you hope she is), she should stick to classic silhouettes as opposed to designs that are trendy or costumey.

The ideal dress is of course one that accentuates your most attractive features and minimizes any jiggling, bumps, or bulges. Many brides are open to selecting dresses that are the same color and fabric yet varied in style (say, a strapless, a halter, and a short sleeve), so that a bridesmaid can choose the one that's most flattering to her particular body type. Brides over thirty often lean toward this option. Most likely, they know what it's like to feel some sort of insecurity about their bodies and want to be certain that their bridesmaids feel attractive and completely comfortable in their dresses.

If you've been asked to be maid of honor, note that you might be expected to wear a slightly different style of gown than the rest of the bridesmaids. Perhaps it will have a distinctive neckline or come in a unique but complementary color.

If you're given style options, consider the following suggestions to find a cut that works best for your body type.

SLIM AND PETITE. The empire waist, in which the seam hits above the natural waistline or just below the bust, is the most flattering style for women with smaller frames because it creates the illusion of a long torso. A column or sheath has a similar lengthening effect. On the other hand, an elaborate ball gown tends to overwhelm a petite figure.

HOURGLASS. Dresses with a halter neckline help balance a woman with a curvy lower body, and a full skirt will accentuate a tiny waist. A two-piece with a corset top and long skirt will work well if your bust is smaller than your hips. However, straight designs or form-fitting bias cuts (in which the fabric is cut diagonally) will magnify the hips and bottom.

FULL FIGURE. For a voluptuous body, an A-line gown, which flares out from the waist, is ideal. Ruching around the midsection can hide a round tummy, and vertical seams have an overall slimming effect. Sheaths, mermaid gowns, and other body-hugging styles should be avoided.

AMPLE BUST. A V-shape or scoop neckline will flatter a woman with a generous bust. A strapless gown also looks great on this figure but will likely not offer enough support, unless you have the proper shapewear (for more on undergarments, see What Lies Beneath, page 67). Try to steer clear of dresses with high necklines or boat necklines—they'll only make your breasts appear larger.

THICK ARMS. If you're uncomfortable baring your upper arms, long or three-quarter-length sleeves will help conceal them. Otherwise, a wrap, shawl, or cropped jacket can be the perfect cover-up.

Color Cues

If the bride is undecided on the color for the bridesmaids' gowns, suggest that she first consider her ceremony and reception décor. The dresses should complement, not clash with, the venue's color scheme as well as reflect the formality of the wedding. For example, pastels are best for an outdoor or daytime wedding, while crimson, plum, and navy are more appropriate for an elegant evening wedding. Even black bridesmaids' dresses, once considered taboo, will perfectly complement a sophisticated, black-tie affair (for more on this choice, see Ladies in Black, opposite). If the bride has asked for your input, take note of the following color considerations, too.

THE SEASON. Deep colors like bordeaux, hunter green, and chocolate work well in the autumn and winter months; in the spring and summer, lighter hues such as rose, lavender, and celadon are ideal.

FIGURE FLATTERY. Darker shades are the most slimming, and solid colors are more likely to flatter full-figured attendants than prints.

AGE APPROPRIATENESS. For bridesmaids in their thirties and forties, it's best not to go with true pinks, since they can look a bit girlish.

SKIN TONE. For colors that flatter most skin tones, you might suggest complex shades like periwinkle and sage rather than bright primary colors.

Remember that traditional brides tend to favor the monochromatic look of having all bridesmaids in the same

··· Ladies in Black ···

A black bridesmaid gown? Absolutely! In the past, dressing female attendants in black was frowned upon; black was thought to be too funeral parlor-ish for a happy occasion like a wedding. Today, not only is black considered appropriate, it's become a popular choice for chic evening weddings.

To erase any lingering somber connotations, here are some ways to make ebony gowns less drab and more fab.

- Carry a bouquet of either pale-pink anemones or yellow roses and mango calla lilies.

- Add a contrasting sash in a hue matching the bride's color scheme.

- Opt for embellishments—a beaded neckline, sequined bodice, or satin trim—or add a crystal brooch.

- Slip on gold or silver shoes, or go for a bold look with a bright shoe (fire-engine red anyone?).

Note that a little black dress looks equally good against fair, medium, and dark skin tones. Plus it's a bridesmaid dress you really can wear again and again and again.

gown, while modern brides will often mix things up with complementary colors or different shades of the same color. Any of these looks will turn out fantastic in photos.

Fabulous Fabrics

The fabric of the bridesmaids' gowns is just as important as the style and color. The formality of the wedding, the season, and the time of day are all important factors to consider when choosing the right dress fabric. If the bride has asked for your advice or if you're shopping for yourself, keep the following seasonal style tips in mind.

FORMAL EVENING. Nighttime galas call for satin or silk—it's worth noting, however, that silk charmeuse is difficult for most women to wear because of the cling factor.

DAYTIME AND/OR SUMMER. Lightweight chiffon and organza dresses are most suitable for daytime or warm-weather nuptials.

WINTER AND/OR BLACK-TIE. Velvet is a decadent option for a black-tie winter wedding, and cotton is an obvious choice for a casual seaside ceremony. Avoid linen, which wrinkles without provocation, at all costs.

These days many brides are choosing to celebrate their heritage, the groom's heritage, or a combination of Western and international traditions by having a multicultural wedding. And an obvious way to incorporate ethnic rituals and customs is through the wedding party's attire.

- If the couple wants an African-inspired wedding, the bridesmaids could wear embroidered African shawls with their gowns in purple and gold—the colors of African royalty.

- For a wedding with Spanish flair, red and black bridesmaid dresses with flamenco-style ruffled hems would be a fitting touch.

- A Japanese wedding might call for female attendants in brightly colored kimonos; bridesmaids in silk cheongsams would be ideal for a Chinese wedding; and handmade beaded saris would perfectly complement an Indian wedding.

Ethnic wedding attire not only looks gorgeous in pictures, it also gives attendants and guests a chance to experience a different culture for a day—in a respectful manner.

"I like to compare being a bridesmaid with being the backup singer in a band. Once when I was matron of honor, the bride's wedding party (bride included) showed up just minutes before the ceremony—they weren't even dressed in their finery and still had to do their hair. But, as most shows do, the wedding did go on." —Karon

WHAT LIES BENEATH

No matter what dress style you'll be wearing, the right undergarments are crucial to getting that completely put-together look. And don't forget, as a member of the bridal party, many eyes will be on you, especially during the ceremony: you won't want unsightly bulges, visible panty lines, an unsupportive bra, or—heaven forbid!—any portion of your lingerie peeking out of your dress. Here are a few guidelines to consider when selecting your under-the-dress attire.

OPT FOR NUDE. If your dress is a light color, err on the side of caution by choosing undergarments that are nude rather than white or colored. Nudes won't show through at all, but white and other colors might.

SELECT SEAMLESS. A fitted dress calls for seamless underwear. Choose a French-cut panty, which is cut high on the legs, rather than a thong, which can be unflattering in a bottom-skimming gown. Have curves? Then shapewear from top to bottom is in order. Brands such as Spanx offer supportive pieces that will cinch your waist, flatten your tummy, and lift your bottom—they are so fabulous you'll wonder where they've been all your life.

CHOOSE STRAPLESS FOR BARE SHOULDERS. For a dress that is low cut or has spaghetti straps, a strapless bra is the obvious choice. Small-breasted women can also wear a padded adhesive bra. If you're busty, you'll need a strapless with extra support—or better yet, try a lightweight torso-hugging bustier.

GO CONVERTIBLE. A convertible bra, which comes with detachable straps that can be arranged in various ways, is your best bet for a halter dress or one with a low back. These multitaskers can also be adjusted to a racerback style to accommodate a high neckline.

PREVENT A SLIP. Finally, if you're stuck wearing a dress with a plunging neckline despite your best efforts to guide the bride's selection process, choose a demi-cup bra, which covers half of each breast and ensures no peekaboo moments.

ACCESSORIZE ME

Once you've got your dress, it's time to pick out shoes, handbags, coverups, and any other accessories the bride would like her attendants to wear.

COVER-UPS. Some religious ceremonies, such as Catholic church weddings, require brides and bridesmaids to cover their shoulders; in these situations, a wrap, evening jacket (like a cropped bolero), or a shrug (which wraps snugly around your upper arms) may also be part of your wedding attire. Many bridesmaids collections conveniently offer these add-ons in a matching color and fabric for your dress. But even if they're not required, cover-ups can add a touch of class to any formal affair.

GLOVES. The bride may also opt for a vintage look by adorning bridesmaids with wrist-length gloves or opera gloves extending to the elbows, which would go nicely with tea-length or ballerina dresses.

"I've been a maid of honor five times and a bridesmaid ten times and counting. . . . I even wore the exact same dress six times—it must have been the color and style of the moment!"—Kristen

HANDBAGS. Each bridesmaid isn't required to carry the same bag; after all, your purse won't be seen until the reception. Nonetheless, when choosing your bag, think small. Consider a clutch in the same fabric as your gown and in a neutral color—such as silver, gold, champagne, or black.

JEWELRY. You will want to check with the bride before choosing your wedding jewelry. She may have certain preferences—studs versus chandelier earrings, for example—or she may be planning on gifting you and the other attendants with your wedding bling at the bridesmaids' luncheon.

SHOES. When it comes to choosing the shoes you'll wear with your gown, brides typically fall into one of two categories. She may give you a general description of the style and color she prefers and then leave the rest up to you. For example, her only request may be for you to wear a pair of silver strappy sandals or basic black heels. On the other hand, if she's a stickler about having everything perfectly in sync, particularly if she's chosen knee-length dresses that put your feet on display, she may pick out the exact pair she wants you to wear. But if she insists on the dyed-to-match satin pumps, at least attempt to dissuade her!

GET MEASURED

After the dresses are chosen, the next step is to get professionally measured. Any department store will offer this service, often free of charge. Just make sure the person doing the measuring is a seamstress as opposed to an untrained associate. This appointment is important because sizes vary from label to label. If you know your measurements, you can cross-reference them with the dress manufacturer's size chart to make sure you don't order a dress that's two sizes too big or too small.

For the appointment, bring the undergarments you plan to wear with your dress (any layers will make a difference), and then request the following measurements: bust, waist, hip, and dress length.

The Perfect Fit

Even if you've gotten your measurements and ordered the gown in the size closest to them on the manufacturer's size chart, your dress will likely still need to be altered to some degree. The bride may set up these appointments (preferably two) or she may rely on you to book them on your

··· THE PREGNANT BRIDESMAID ···

If you're expecting when asked be a bridesmaid (or discover afterward that you're pregnant and the bride still wants you to be her attendant), take some time to think about whether you should participate. The bride and other bridesmaids will most likely be sensitive to the fact that you may not be able to spend long hours shopping for gowns and accessories. And keep in mind that there have been many pregnant bridesmaids before you who didn't let their expanding bellies get in the way of standing up for a close friend or relative.

So, if you decide to participate, what does a pregnant bridesmaid wear? A dress with an empire waist (one that hits right below the bustline) will leave plenty of room for a growing tummy. Or talk to the bride about opting for a maternity dress in the same color or fabric as the other bridesmaid dresses. Don't worry: there are plenty of flattering styles to choose from. It's a good idea to order the dress in a size larger than you think it will need to be—it's much easier for a seamstress to take a dress in than to let it out.

Also, you should have your final fitting and alterations done as close to the wedding as possible to ensure a proper fit. In terms of shoes, dressy flats will be best. What's most important is that you're as comfortable as possible.

own. Either way, you should allow plenty of time—at least four to six weeks—for alterations. Out-of-town bridesmaids will need to make sure they receive their dresses in time to schedule at least one formal fitting before the wedding. Again, at this appointment you'll need to wear your bridal lingerie and bring the shoes you'll be wearing (or at least a pair with the same heel height).

CH. 4

PREWEDDING EVENTS

Let the parties begin! A wedding is a huge occasion with lots of smaller celebrations leading up to it. As a bridesmaid, you'll have to cohost a couple of these, namely the shower and bachelorette party. Plus, the bride will likely organize a small party for you and the rest of the attendants, most often called the "bridesmaids' luncheon." It's her way of thanking you all for your contributions, love, and support, and for standing up for her on one of the most joyous days of her life.

THE BRIDAL SHOWER

This gift-giving party is traced back to a sixteenth- or seventeenth-century Dutch tale about a woman whose father disapproved of the man she loved and withheld her dowry when they married. In response, the woman's female friends got together to offer the bride-to-be all the clothing and household goods she'd need to maintain a home with her future husband. Following in that tradition, in Colonial times bridal-shower gifts filled a new bride's hope chest with the essentials needed to prepare her for marriage—and, in later years, the occasion helped her collect trousseau items (bridal attire and lingerie). Times have certainly changed, but housewares and pretty little things are still frequently given as shower gifts.

Traditionally, the maid or matron of honor hosts the shower with the help of the other bridesmaids, and costs are split evenly. Relatives of the bride should never be the ones hosting the party—it sends a message that the family is soliciting presents on the bride's behalf. If the bride's sister is the honor attendant, she can certainly still help with the planning, as can other family members, but the family name should be left off the invitations. The menu is often reminiscent of a Victorian-style tea party with such light bites as finger sandwiches, petit fours, and scones.

The highlight is often the opening of the gifts. At this time, the honor attendant should be ready to jot down which guest gave which gift, plus any notable comments or gestures the bride or gift-giver makes. Another bridesmaid should make sure the cards stay with the corresponding packages, which will help make writing thank-you notes a breeze for the bride.

"For my sister-in-law's shower, she had wanted something very sophisticated, so I threw her a high tea at a beautiful tea shop. She told me it was her dream shower, exactly what she wanted— so I was thrilled to be able to give that to her." — Jeanine

Who Attends?

The shower typically includes the bride's closest friends and family members. You shouldn't expect to invite every female on the wedding guest list. If the shower is a surprise, which it often is, you'll need to gather a guest list from the bride's mother or her immediate family—just make sure it includes the groom's close relatives, too. You wouldn't want to unknowingly offend anyone. If the bride's in the loop about her shower, she'll be able to provide you with the guest list. It's important to note that anyone invited to the shower must be invited to the wedding—no exceptions!

Planning Like a Pro

Most bridal showers are relaxed gabfests complete with plenty of laughs, savory nibbles and delicious desserts, and maybe a parlor game or two, all leading up to a gift-opening extravaganza. However, it does take a bit of creativity to ensure that a fantastic time is had by all. Here, celebrity party planner David Tutera offers some bridal shower basics.

PICK A PLACE. When choosing the venue (whether it's at someone's home or in a public space), the bridesmaid should think about a few key points. First, what would the bride like? Would she prefer a sophisticated high tea at a fancy restaurant, where the ladies will lunch and she will open gifts? Would she rather play loud games in a great hotel suite? Or would she be more comfortable hanging out in her best friend's living room? Wherever you hold the shower, make sure the venue echoes the bride's taste and personality—and make sure it fits in the budget. Other crucial factors to consider are the head count and size of the space, as well as its proximity to where everyone lives or will be staying.

WORK IN A THEME. The "gift-theme" idea can be a fun way to stock the bride and groom with household essentials, such as kitchenware or linens. For example, an "around-the-clock" shower assigns guests to specific times of the day, and their gifts should reflect their designated hour (a guest with 1 A.M. might give a pair of nighttime eye masks or a piece of lingerie). Try to choose a theme that will really benefit the bride, again keeping her personality and style in mind. If she already has a well-supplied kitchen but could use a fully-stocked bar, consider having each guest bring a bar-related gift, such as a beautiful ice bucket, luxurious serving trays, high-end brands of liquor, and custom-monogrammed coasters.

··· Boys Allowed ···

A coed bridal shower? It's not out of the question. Brides who aren't too concerned about following tradition may express a desire to have their groom attend the shower—and that means male attendants and the significant others of female invitees would also be invited.

Obviously, letting the boys in means tweaking the agenda. A "couple's shower," a.k.a. the "Jack and Jill," should be a dinner party or cookout rather than an afternoon tea, and there should be gender-neutral activities. Boy-versus-girl trivia games might help break the ice and assure the guys that they won't have to endure copious amounts of girl talk.

You can still play with themes but these should revolve around something the couple enjoys. For example, if the bride and groom are film buffs, you could decorate a room with movie posters; serve buckets of popcorn and theater treats like Raisinets, Junior Mints, Lemonheads, and Red Hots; and perhaps set up a looping montage of clips from their favorite flicks on a projector screen.

As for gifts, stick with items that both guests of honor would appreciate: barware, an espresso maker, or a breakfast-in-bed gift set. Also, make it clear from the shower invitations that both genders will be attending, so guests will know what to expect.

"Being a bridesmaid is a huge honor—and with that privilege comes a huge responsibility. When you're chosen as a bridesmaid, especially a maid of honor, the bride is not only showing how close you are to her, but that she trusts you to handle the biggest day of her life."

—*Elizabeth*

To work a bar theme into the bridal shower décor, turn paper drink coasters into place cards, make custom-imprinted cocktail napkins, and concoct a signature cocktail to match the look and style of the shower. You can even arrange flowers in beautiful champagne buckets to display on the tables.

BRING ON THE ENTERTAINMENT. Activities like The Newlywed Game or a wedding version of Scattergories can help people mingle and relax, but keep in mind that there are other ways to entertain the crowd. For something a little different, hire a handwriting analyst, a mentalist, a henna artist, or even a caricaturist.

IT'S ALL IN THE DETAILS. Another way to honor the bride at the shower is to gather party favors that reflect her personality. Is she a gym buff? Give each guest an adorable pink jump rope, an eco-friendly water bottle, or even a yoga mat in a color that matches your décor. Does the bride live on caffeine? Hand out gift certificates to a favorite coffee chain. Does everyone know the bride is a fanatical list-maker? Have list pads made for each guest. A bridal shower is a great opportunity to have fun with the favors and give guests something truly unique.

You're Invited

When it comes to setting a shower date, plan for a day anywhere between six months to a week before the wedding. If there will be many out-of-town guests, mail the invitations at least two months in advance to give people time to make travel arrangements. Otherwise, it's okay to send them four to six weeks before the shower. Designate a date for RSVPs. If you don't hear from everyone by then, follow up with a phone call or friendly e-mail.

Once you have the basics covered (the date, the venue, and the type of party you're throwing), you're ready to choose the stationery. Your invitations should reflect the formality of the wedding and set the tone for the shower. For example, an ink-printed invitation with a whimsical illustration of a bride's gown hanging from an armoire would be perfectly appropriate for a casual party. The invite is also a way to introduce the party theme. And, unlike with the wedding invitations, it is acceptable to include information on the couple's gift registry.

Shower Gift Guide

A lovely tradition at many bridal showers has been for the bridesmaids to present the bride with a sterling silver

··· AN ECO-FRIENDLY FETE ···

If the bride is environmentally conscious, she would no doubt appreciate a bridal shower that reflected her global views. Here are a few simple ways to add some green sensibilities to the festivities.

- Hold the shower outdoors—in a garden, at a park, on the beach—wherever the beauty of nature can serve as the décor.

- Send invitations made of recycled paper or natural fibers and printed with soy ink.

- Hire a caterer that uses organic and/or locally grown ingredients.

- Find a baker that makes vegan cupcakes and display them on a vintage cupcake tower.

- Avoid using disposable napkins, cups, and utensils.

- Suggest that guests give eco-friendly and socially conscious gifts, such as organic cotton towels, recycled-glass serving bowls, or fair-trade scarves, shawls, or bags benefiting women and children in developing countries. Another option is to ask guests to contribute to the bride's favorite environmental charity.

decorative tray engraved with each of their initials. Other group gifts could include a pair of theater or concert tickets, a spa gift certificate, or travel gear. When it comes to individual gifts, the party's theme will guide you to a specific gift category. Otherwise, the couple's gift registry is the natural place to begin. Try relating your shower gift to your wedding gift; for instance, fancy dessert plates could precede a nice bakeware set. Lingerie is another common shower gift, but be careful not to confuse the shower with the bachelorette party. Boudoir items should be tasteful, especially if the bride is on the modest side. And remember that her mother and perhaps a grandmother or two will also be watching her unwrap her presents.

As for how much to spend on a shower gift, anything in the range of twenty-five to seventy-five dollars is appropriate. Give what you can afford. Or present the bride with something priceless—homemade gifts like a scrapbook, crocheted scarf, or handcrafted charm bracelet are personalized and thoughtful. DIY not your thing? Browse the gift ideas below for inspiration.

- Silver frame engraved with her new initials
  (only do this if you know for sure that
  the bride will be taking her husband's name)

- Tea set and tea pot
- Linen napkins and napkin rings
- Crystal champagne flutes
- Cashmere blankets
- Coffeemaker
- China
- Cake plate
- Serving platters
- Membership to a wine-, fruit-, or flower-of-the-month club
- One-year museum membership
- Gift basket filled with scented candles and pampering bath products
- Honeymoon travel books (if you know where the couple is going)

Bridal Shower Timeline

Having trouble keeping track of all your bridal shower to-dos? Here's a checklist that should help put it all in perspective. The maid or matron of honor will be handling many of these tasks, but you can note here which tasks have been delegated to you. Refer to this list often as you're planning the shower, and of course tweak specific times and tasks as needed.

Six-Plus Months Before the Wedding

- Start planning. Talk to the other bridesmaids and decide if the bride would prefer a surprise shower or if she'd rather be in the loop. Decide where to host the festivities, whether there will be a theme, and what type of food and entertainment you want to provide. Make restaurant or catering hall reservations, if applicable.
- Set the date. Depending on the number of out-of-town guests, the event can be held from six months to one week prior to the wedding.
- Create the guest list. Ask the bride or her immediate relatives who should receive an invitation. Remember that everyone on the list must also be invited to the wedding.

Two Months Before the Shower

- Send save-the-date cards. Mailing them four to six weeks before the event is especially important if some invitees need time to make travel arrangements. If the majority of guests live out of town, consider sending the formal invites at this time.
- Discuss the budget with the other bridesmaids and settle on a single amount each attendant will need to contribute to help pay for the party.
- Decide on the theme, style, and activities. Hold a

brainstorming session to finalize details concerning the decorations, favors, menu, and activities. The honor attendant should use this time to assign specific tasks.

- Make any necessary reservations, whether at the venue you've chosen or for caterers if the shower will be hosted in someone's home.
- Research and book the entertainment and/or talent for the occasion, if necessary.

One Month Before the Shower

- Mail the formal invitations. The invites should include information about the gift theme, if there is one, and where the couple is registered.
- Shop for the decorations and/or other party props.
- Order the flowers, favors, and/or any personalized elements.

Two Weeks Before the Shower

- Shop for your shower gift or finalize arrangements for the group gift.
- Create a food and drink shopping list if the party will be held at someone's home.
- Confirm RSVPs.

"At a bridal shower I planned, the bride insisted on wearing a tiara. The maid of honor and I drove to six stores in search of one we thought the bride might like, but when she saw the tiara we chose, she cried! A photo of the maid of honor (the bride's best friend) placing the tiara in her hair turned out to be one of the best photos from the entire wedding."—Emily

One Week Before the Shower

- Confirm restaurant or catering hall reservations.
- Confirm flower and food delivery times.
- Buy groceries, if necessary.

One Day Before the Shower

- Do any food prep if the party will be held at someone's home.
- Assemble favors and/or decorations.
- Run any last-minute errands (confirm cake pickup times, arrange the party space if the shower will be held in your home, etc.) and make sure all bridesmaids have completed their to-dos.

THE BACHELORETTE PARTY

What makes for a great bachelorette party? Pretty much anything that'll get all the girls fired up—and give the bride a chance to relax and just have a blast with her girlfriends before she bids adieu to the single life. Whether the group is going out to paint the town red or staying in for a low-key living room soiree, the point is to have fun.

The bachelorette party isn't structured like the bridal shower, but it does require a good amount of planning. The maid of honor should take the lead, but she should feel free to solicit help from eager, fun-loving bridesmaids. If you're partying at home, you'll need to arrange for refreshments and activities. Compile a shopping list that includes decorations, snacks, drinks, and games, and divvy it up among the bridesmaids. Decide who will be in charge of the music or other entertainment.

Will it be a girls' night out? If so, create an itinerary, make reservations and/or purchase tickets in advance, and schedule all necessary travel arrangements if there's a chauffeured limo or party bus in the works. If you're planning a pub crawl, ask around about drink specials and let the bartenders know why you're there—you might get a comped drink or other freebies out of it. A safety note: be sure to leave the list of clubs or bars you'll be visiting with a trusted friend or relative, and assign someone to be the designated driver or keep the number of a car service handy. Figure out total costs as soon as possible so all attendees will know ahead of time how much they'll need to contribute. Remember, this event gets split up among everyone, bridesmaids and other guests alike.

And don't forget about the props. Novelty bridal accessories, such as a white feather boa or a mini veil attached to a sparkly tiara, will make the bride stand out in a crowd. Presents aren't required like they are for the bridal shower, but racy lingerie and gag gifts (naughty paraphernalia or sex books, for example) are often passed around. As long as you know the bride will be a good sport about it and you're keeping things age-appropriate (i.e., not too juvenile for a mature bride), let your imagination run wild. After all, making the bride blush is part of the fun.

Who Attends?

Just as with the shower, anyone invited to the bachelorette party has to be invited to the wedding. It's uncouth to invite your neighbor or coworker simply because you think she'd add some life to the party. Older relatives like the bride's mother or her great aunt Mary should probably be left off the guest list—most definitely if you're headed out for a night of debauchery. And it's best to keep the party small; try to keep it to fewer than twenty people.

Set a Date

The bachelorette party can be held from a month to a week before the wedding—but never the night before. You can't risk the bride and her bridesmaids looking red-eyed and puffy-faced and suffering from hangovers and lack of sleep at the ceremony. Your first step is to sit down with the bride about three months before you set your plans in motion and ask her what kind of bash she wants—or doesn't want. It's okay to surprise her with some of the details but pay attention to her basic requirements. Then check in with the best man to find out when the guys are having the groom's bachelor party. It's ideal to schedule them on the same night, so there's no chance the bride or groom will be at home stewing over what the other is doing. E-mail the rest of the bridesmaids and other close friends of the bride about the final date to ensure they don't have scheduling conflicts.

Since the bachelorette party is informal, store-bought invitations are fine. You can also design your own using desktop publishing software. Or send an e-mail invitation with a fun image of the night's theme—martini glasses if it's a cocktail party, girls dancing beneath a disco ball, or a quirky Queen of Hearts if a poker night is in store. If you'll just be hanging out at a local bar, invites might not even be necessary. Calling guests a couple of weeks before the event will suffice.

··· The Ultimate Girls' Getaway ···

These days, some bridesmaids are taking the idea of the bachelorette party to whole new level. They're extending it beyond the one night and turning it into a weekend trip to some fabulous destination.

Before planning the girls' great escape—whether it involves cruising the Strip in Vegas, sipping tequila in Cancun, or skiing in Aspen—the honor attendant should make sure all the bridesmaids are on board. You'll need to give them ample time to save up for transportation and hotel accommodations, if necessary. Depending on the time of year, you can often find great off-peak packages on vacations and cruises. Check with a travel agent about special group rates on flights and hotels. For a weekend trip, it's best to settle on a destination that takes no more than three hours to get to by plane (you don't want to waste precious time on travel alone).

Before you go, research as much as you can about your hotel or resort, and find the best places to eat, drink, shop, and get pampered. Create an information packet and itinerary for the ladies so everyone knows the plan. And don't forget to exchange cell phone digits and room numbers with one another.

Girls Just Wanna Have Fun

The best part about a bachelorette party is that your options are endless. You can meet up at the bride's favorite Spanish tapas bar, tear up the dance floor at a popular nightclub, get glammed up for a rock concert, rent a private room for a hilarious evening of karaoke, or arrange a bar-hopping scavenger hunt that includes a list of mischievous missions you have in store for the bride. Here are a few other fabulous ways to entertain the girls.

IT'S COCKTAIL TIME. Grab the girls, dress to the nines, and spend the evening at a cool jazz club or swanky cocktail lounge. Or create your own *Sex and the City*–type party at home. Mix up cosmopolitans, mojitos, or Long Island iced teas, or create a signature cocktail like the "Blushing Bride" (add four parts champagne to a flute filled with one part peach schnapps and one part grenadine syrup). Serve the mixed drinks with crudités and dip, cheese and crackers, or a few retro snacks like Swedish meatballs, pigs in blankets, and deviled eggs. Set the mood with dim lighting and a playlist of lounge music.

CASINO NIGHT. Viva Las Vegas! Book the bachelorette party at a casino resort for access to great restaurants, live shows, and concerts—and of course complimentary drinks in the game rooms. Gambling parties also give you the chance to walk away with some extra cash . . . but put down only what you can afford to lose. Book a slot of rooms for the night, so you don't have to worry about getting home safely after dark.

WINE AND DINE. Is the bride a foodie? Giving her a culinary experience might be the way to go. Consider reserving a table at a restaurant that offers a five-course tasting menu and wine pairing. Or if someone in the bridal party is a great cook, try this at home. Ask a wine expert (a restaurant sommelier or wine shop dealer) for wines that would pair well with the items on your menu.

Fondue parties can also be a lot of fun. Either go to your favorite fondue place or buy mini pots to do the dipping at home. Start off with cheese fondue, then move on to the main course (use a flavorful broth, wine, or olive oil to cook raw meats, poultry, or seafood in fondue pots), and end the meal with dessert fondue made with chocolate and cream. Each bridesmaid can bring her share of the accompaniments—chopped up vegetables and fruits (strawberries are a must), cubes of French bread and pound cake, marshmallows, and bite-sized cookies.

"I was lucky to snag a reservation at a hot new tapas restaurant for my best friend's bachelorette party. On the day of the party, I walked up to the hostess and told her I had a reservation. As she's telling us that they don't take reservations, the manager came over to welcome us. The look on the hostess's face was priceless—as was providing my best friend with the ultimate V.I.P. evening." —Melissa

A DAY AT THE SPA. How about a bachelorette party that not only relieves stress but also gets you gorgeous for that walk down the aisle? Consider a spa party—it's a way to literally let loose. Imagine plush robes, pampering massages, soothing facials, and beauty treatments galore. Choose a day spa with a full-service menu—from body scrubs and mud wraps to manicures and pedicures—that can accommodate a small group. Set up appointments far in advance and confirm them a few days beforehand. If you'd rather have a beauty team come to you, check out a mobile day spa. Many have packages that include appetizers and champagne.

Bachelorette Party Timeline

Need a system to help keep track of all your bachelorette party to-dos? Here's a checklist that should do the trick. Refer to this list often as you're planning the party, adjusting specific times and tasks as needed.

Three-Plus Months Before the Wedding

- Start planning. Ask the bride what kind of party she wants—a raucous night on the town or a low-key girls' night in. Would she prefer a jazz lounge, comedy club, concert, or casino? Or is she game for a bachelorette weekend getaway?

- Set the date. The maid of honor should discuss the timing with the best man, the organizer of the bachelor party, since both events should coincide. Shoot for a date that's one month to one week before the wedding. Remember, the day before the wedding is off limits.
- Create the guest list. Consult the bride and try to keep the number of invites to fewer than twenty. Remember that everyone on the list must also be invited to the wedding.

Two Months Before the Party

- Send out casual save-the-dates (via e-mail is fine) to find out if there are any major scheduling conflicts among the invitees.
- Discuss the budget with the other bridesmaids and settle on a single amount each guest will need to contribute to help pay for the festivities. If you're planning a big trip to a faraway destination, inform guests of the total cost a few months in advance so they can make an informed decision when they RSVP.
- Decide on the theme, style, and activities. Hold a

brainstorming session to discuss the game plan and the surprises you'll have in store for the bride.

- Make any necessary reservations, order show or concert tickets, and/or finalize hotel and transportation details.
- Research and book the entertainment and/or talent for the evening.

One Month Before the Party

- Send the invitations (via e-mail is fine). Timing is especially important if you need to get final head counts for activities that require reservations or if some invitees need to make travel arrangements. Otherwise, sending invites or making calls two weeks before the party is acceptable. Be sure to inform guests exactly how much money they'll need to contribute toward the party.
- If barhopping is on the agenda, devise an itinerary for the night and share it with a trusted friend or relative who won't be attending. Call the bars to ask about drink specials or other bachelorette party freebies.

One Week Before the Party

- For an at-home soiree, finalize the night's menu, music, and activities. Create a shopping list (including games, decorations, naughty party props, food, and drinks) and divvy it up among the bridesmaids.
- Buy bachelorette party novelty items for the bride (such as a "Bride" cap, mini veil, tiara, or white feather boa) if she'll enjoy them.
- Confirm RSVPs.
- Confirm food delivery times and entertainment bookings, if necessary.
- Confirm chauffeured limo, party bus, or other transportation arrangements.

One Day Before the Party

- Remind guests of the meeting times and places and/or distribute an itinerary.
- Do any food prep for an at-home party. Make sure you have plenty of ice for drinks.
- Run any last-minute errands (change camera battery or purchase extra memory card, arrange the party space if the festivities will be held in your home, etc.) and make sure all bridesmaids have completed their to-dos.

THE BRIDESMAIDS' LUNCHEON

The bride hosts this intimate gathering as her way of showing her appreciation for all that the bridesmaids have done to help her prepare for the big day. It's during this occasion that she typically presents each bridesmaid with a gift. It might be a piece of jewelry she'd like you to wear to the wedding (a pair of earrings or a necklace) or a monogrammed jewelry box, frame, or handbag. In lieu of a luncheon, the bride may decide to organize a high tea, a casual dinner, or even a happy hour for her attendants.

Ladies Who Lunch

The bridesmaids' lunch may be held a couple days before the wedding or on the morning or afternoon of the wedding. It's a perfect opportunity to reflect on the past few months and get everyone excited about the fact that the big day has finally arrived. The luncheon typically includes only the bride's attendants as well as the junior bridesmaids and the flower girl. Because it's such a casual event, you may or may not get a formal invitation. Although the event is being held in your honor, the bridesmaids can also use this time to present the bride with your group wedding gift (if there is one). Or perhaps unveil little trinkets that represent her something old, something new, something borrowed, and/or something blue (if the bride hasn't already chosen them). For example, one bridesmaid could lend the bride the veil she wore at her wedding and another could lend a sapphire pendant or pin, which the bride could secure to her sash or the underside of her gown. The maid or matron of honor might also offer the bride some words of encouragement, and any married maids can share what they've learned about how to sustain a happy, healthy marriage.

CH. *5*

THE REHEARSAL

You know the drill——or you will soon enough. On the eve of the wedding, the entire bridal party (plus readers, ushers, and the parents of the bride and groom) comes together to get direction on what to do from the moment they arrive at the wedding until it's time to whoop it up at the reception. The officiant will be guiding the ceremony proceedings, and you can also expect the photographer, videographer, and DJ (if he or she will be the evening's master of ceremonies) to be on hand to scope out the venues and discuss logistics, such as the timing of specific songs, dances, and speeches. If you have any questions or concerns about any aspect of the wedding-day formalities (especially if the wedding involves religious or cultural traditions that are unfamiliar to you), now is the time to clear them up.

The run-throughs are hardly the most exciting part of the prewedding activities, but there is something to look forward to. After all is said and done, you'll get to enjoy a "practice" reception during the rehearsal dinner, courtesy of the groom's family.

PRACTICE MAKES PERFECT

On an occasion as momentous as a wedding, the goal is for things to go as smoothly as possible. And the only way to ensure nothing goes horribly awry is to practice, practice, practice. The rehearsal dinner is a great opportunity to make sure everyone knows where he or she is supposed to be, to find out how to deal with any last-minute glitches, and to ease any prewedding nerves. Because the officiant, the couple, and the rest of the bridal party are counting on you to be ready and on time, try to arrive earlier than expected. But don't leave without eating a protein-rich snack in case the rehearsal runs longer than expected.

Places Everyone

You've got to know your cues. At the rehearsal, you'll find out the order in which you'll be walking down the aisle, which groomsman will be your escort, where and how you'll be standing at the altar, and how you'll be walking back up the aisle. You'll also learn where to stand on the receiving line, if there is one. Expect at least two practice runs during the rehearsal. See page 124 for more on what to expect during the ceremony.

Be Prepared

The rehearsal is the time to review your wedding-day responsibilities. For instance, remember that you or another bridesmaid needs to bring copies of the ceremony readings in case someone forgets or misplaces his or her copy. Keep them in your purse or someplace where they can be easily retrieved. The maid of honor will practice handing off the ring to the bride during the ceremony, so it may be left with her at this time until the following day. It's a good idea for you and/or the other bridesmaids to send her a quick text message on the morning of the wedding to remind her not to leave home without the precious cargo.

Among the most unpredictable aspects of the wedding will be how the young children in the wedding party will behave. In Chapter 1, you learned the importance of taking the time to establish a bond with child attendants so they're comfortable interacting with you and with one another. But, of course, nothing's foolproof. If you can't seem to convince a stubborn ring bearer to walk down the aisle,

❧ You Want Me to Do *What?* ❧

Certain brides have moments when their frustration gets the best of them and they may say or do things they wouldn't normally do. Whether you blame it on the stress of dealing with dueling family members, frazzled nerves, or maybe lack of sleep, these moments are all that more likely to occur the closer you get to the day of the wedding. During one of these episodes, it's possible that you could be asked to do something that goes way above and beyond your bridesmaids' duties. In these cases, it's perfectly okay to graciously decline the request. Remember, you're her bridesmaid, not her servant. You may accept some less than pleasant tasks out of the goodness of your heart, but you're certainly not required to do any of the following favors.

- Spend an unreasonable amount of time on tedious tasks. A few hours spent affixing personalized labels to mini bottles of wine is one thing, but an entire weekend doing this plus six other things is quite another.

- Arrange centerpieces. If cost is a factor, you can offer to help the bride research affordable floral designers.

- Get involved in serious family conflicts—it's best to stay neutral in these situations.

"My best friend's wedding was held in the most stunning Catholic church with vaulted ceilings and a super-long aisle. As I walked down the aisle during the rehearsal, you could hear the click of my heels echo throughout the entire place. When I got to the altar, the priest looked at me and said, 'Don't worry, the ceremony music will help drown that out.'"

—Miranda

try a little positive reinforcement. Tell him you'll show him something cool or give him a mom-approved treat if he does a good job as ring bearer—just make sure you follow through on your promise or you'll lose the trust you're so desperately trying to gain.

REHEARSAL DINNER

The rehearsal dinner, typically hosted by the groom's parents, is the last time before the wedding that members of the wedding party and immediate family members will have a chance to wish the couple well. This celebratory dinner is often as formal as the reception. It's the perfect time to mingle with all of the other VIP guests, so you won't be introducing yourself for the first time at the reception. And since introducing guests to the parents and grandparents of the couple is part of your wedding-day duties, this is your chance to find out who's who in the crowd. The bride and groom may also choose to give their attendants and parents small tokens of their appreciation at the rehearsal dinner. And finally, this celebration signals the beginning of the wedding toasting— and perhaps some good-natured roasting.

Cheers!

As the host of the party, the groom's father is typically the first to toast his soon-to-be daughter-in-law and her family. The groom may also say a few words of thanks to everyone in attendance. The bridal-party members are not required to give speeches at this time, but a couple of groomsmen or bridesmaids may choose to, especially if there won't be an opportunity for them to give one on the wedding day. The best man, who will be the designated toastmaster during the reception, will likely offer a toast, and the maid of honor should strongly consider following suit. Your speech can be a chance to deliver a special message to the couple in an intimate setting. You should, however, save your best material for the reception, when more people can hear your sentiments and the emotions of the day will be at a high. For more on speeches and toasts, see page 134.

Cʜ. *6*

THE BIG DAY

The moment everyone has been waiting for has finally arrived. The dress shopping, the fittings, the search for the perfect shoes, the party planning, the late nights spent reassuring the bride that she has everything covered all have brought you to this point. The wedding day is a huge, life-changing event for the bride—and it should be a proud moment for you. Take a moment to check in with the bride. Is she feeling some prewedding jitters? Offer a few of the following tips to help calm her nerves.

BREATHE EASY. The moment she feels her butterflies coming on, tell her to stand up straight with her arms down and inhale deeply, taking the time to feel the air fill her lungs, and then exhale for a period of ten or twelve seconds. She should repeat this deep-breathing technique until her nervousness subsides.

GO FOR A WALK. Sometimes all you really need to ease your frazzled state is some fresh air. Taking a brisk walk can be meditative, release pent-up nervous energy, and do wonders for your mood.

HUG IT OUT. A simple hug has incredible psychological and physical benefits. The act of embracing stimulates nerve endings that help ease tense muscles and a worried mind. And if the hug is given by a dear friend or relative—that'd be you—all the better the effect!

THINK OF THE GROOM. When the formalities of the wedding become overwhelming, it's easy for a gal to forget the reason she's going through it. Bring the bride back down to earth by reminding her that this day is all about celebrating the love she and the groom share and their commitment to spend the rest of their lives together. Speaking to her soon-to-be husband on the morning of the wedding might be the best cure for her case of nerves—and his too!

Now all that's left for you to do is to get dressed and made up, fulfill your ceremonial duties, and enjoy the celebration that follows.

GETTING READY

Let the beautifying begin! Wedding hair and makeup specialist Stacey Lyn Weinstein (whose wedding clients have included Susan Levine and Robert Downey Jr.) says your beauty regimen should begin several months before the wedding. To prep your skin, get a facial a couple weeks before the wedding, schedule a body scrub the week of the event, and be diligent about using sunscreen to prevent skin damage and irritation caused by free radicals. For beautiful, healthy tresses, get a trim two weeks before the wedding. If it's a summer wedding, protect your hair from the elements by using a deep-conditioning treatment once a week for a month prior to the wedding, but resume your normal routine one week before the "I do"s.

Next it's time to schedule your hair and makeup trial runs. Weinstein says she likes her bridesmaids to visit for the first time two to three months before the wedding (preferably in pairs, so they can go out for a nice meal afterward while they're all dolled up). "This way, you can trim, color, and condition your hair properly leading up to the big day," she says. This schedule will also give you the opportunity to try out a few different looks and make a final decision on the one you like best ahead of time. The last thing you want is for your wedding-day preparations to be stressful as you apply, remove, and re-apply makeup or keep changing your hairstyle because you're unhappy with the look. It's also important to have plenty of ideas ready to share with the hair and makeup artists. Weinstein suggests arriving early to the trial appointment, bringing magazine tear sheets featuring looks you love, and being upfront about the styles you absolutely don't want. However, keep an open mind about new looks, such as hair extensions or a different lip color.

The few hours before the wedding, when all the girls are packed in a small room getting gussied up, can be the most chaotic thus far—but they can also be among the most exciting for the bride and her maids. Hearts are fluttering, adrenaline's rushing, and the time for female-bonding is at its peak. But remember to mind your bridesmaid duties. Prepping the bride is the priority. Make sure her

"During the weekend of my wedding we endured some hiccups (Hurricane Hanna joined us at my outdoor tented reception), but each of my amazing bridesmaids was there to take my mind off things and keep me calm— and to make sure that I remembered to eat!" —Lisa

hair and makeup are just right, help her into her gown, and of course tell her how stunning she looks (because no doubt she's glowing). This is also the time to practice bustling her train. Decide which bridesmaid will do the honors and at what point after the ceremony it will be done. Note that when a dress is bustled properly, the fabric will drape gracefully and the hem will be even all around. Then you can get to the business of making sure you're ready to go.

Reveal Radiant Skin

All eyes will be on the blushing bride as she makes her way down the aisle, but those who precede her will also get their fair share of attention too. So if you've got skin concerns, don't wait until the night before the wedding to deal with them. Here are Weinstein's remedies for a few common problems.

ACNE. Clear up breakouts by getting a professional facial no closer than two weeks before the wedding. For stubborn blemishes (or if you don't usually get facials) start the skin treatments a few months before the event. Want a quick fix? Consider LED light therapy, which is now available in many salons and spas. Also, ask a pro to give you recommendations on the type of acne-fighting products that would work best for your skin, and use an exfoliant as part of your at-home routine.

Dull skin. Removing the dead layers of the skin through exfoliation is the best way to banish dull skin. Exfoliating not only improves the appearance of dull skin, it also helps improve skin issues like redness and dehydration. There are two types of exfoliants, physical and chemical, so choose wisely. Over-the-counter scrubs are physical exfoliants that use abrasive ingredients to slough dead cells from the surface of the skin. They're a good option for women with normal or combination skin. If your skin is oily or acne-prone, chemical exfoliants may work better for you: they loosen the bonds between healthy and dead skin cells by using an acid or an enzyme. Chemical exfoliants include alpha hydroxy acids (AHA), beta hydroxy acids (BHA), retinoids, and chemical peels. Because the active ingredients in chemical exfoliants range from mild to strong, they're appropriate for a wide range of skin types—except extremely sensitive skin.

··· PUT YOUR BEST FACE FORWARD ···

At the makeup trial, you should have experimented with different applications and eventually settled on your complete wedding-day look—so stick with it. The day of the wedding is no time to make last-minute switches! Here are a few final makeup dos and don'ts.

- Do buy the lipstick that you and your makeup artist selected for the wedding.

- Do allow plenty of time for your makeup application so your artist can do her best work.

- Do stash blotting papers in your purse to refresh your makeup or soak up a shiny T-zone during the day.

- Don't get a facial the day of or before the wedding. Chances are your skin will still be a bit irritated, so your makeup won't look its best.

- Don't assume that your makeup artist will be able to cover bruises or tattoos on the spot. Body concealers come in a wide range of shades, so she may not have a product that matches your skin tone. If you want anything covered on your body, give your makeup pro a few days' notice so she can come prepared.

REDNESS. The primary cause of red, irritated skin is dilated capillaries, which give your face a flushed appearance. The best way to prevent redness is to use beauty products that don't contain perfumes or harsh ingredients. Using calming serums and gentle face masks regularly can also help to combat ruddiness.

Have a Good Hair Day

There are so many great hair styles bridesmaids can pull off, from wearing it up to leaving it down or pulling it up halfway. Here's a rundown of some of Weinstein's favorite wedding looks.

ROMANTIC. Create a combination of waves and curls, and wear your hair down or pull it into a side-swept updo.

CLEAN AND CLASSIC. Straighten your hair with a flatiron, apply hair gloss, and then add a skinny headband or gather your hair into a chic low ponytail.

WHIMSICAL. Give your hair tons of waves and pull a few pieces up away from your face; or loosely tie your wavy hair into an off-center ponytail.

GLAMOROUS. If you've got short hair, get Marilyn Monroe's trademark curls by setting your hair in large electric rollers. After removing them, pull one side of your hair back and secure with a small crystal clip.

Dressing the Bride

Slipping into a wedding gown often requires the help of at least two women. Think of the volume, the cathedral-length train (if she has one), and those teeny-tiny buttons and fasteners. Ball gowns will need to be stepped into, so help the bride unbutton or unzip the dress and position it over her shoes. You and another bridesmaid (or the bride's mother) can then hold it open and physically support her as she steps inside and slips into a shoe, one leg at a time. If her dress is a sheath or another style that needs to be slipped over her head, help her hold a towel or scarf over her face so she doesn't get makeup smudges on the dress.

She'll need to feel confident and comfortable in her attire, so once she's dressed and walking around, keep an eye out to make sure nothing is falling down, flipping up, pinching, or constricting. Then do a spot check. If anything's amiss (a torn hem, peekaboo undergarments, a pesky stain), use the emergency kit you so diligently packed to make a quick fix.

THE CEREMONY

After the bride and bridesmaids are finished getting ready, it's time to tackle any preceremony tasks. These could include getting pictures taken; setting out wedding programs; scoping out the venue to make sure the rest of the bridal party is standing by and that the floral arrangements, pew decorations, and other elements are in place; or helping early-arriving guests find their seats. If the reception is being held in an adjoining room, you should also confirm that the cake and extras like an ice sculpture have arrived safely, place cards have been set up at each table, and the guest book and favors are where they need to be. Soon enough, it'll be time for everyone to take their places.

Although religious and civil ceremonies may differ in terms of certain rituals (such as the reciting of blessings), most weddings have the same basic structure, with readings and special musical selections typically blended in as well.

- Processional
- Opening remarks
- Vows
- Ring exchange

- Lighting of a unity candle (if desired)
- Closing remarks
- Pronouncement that the couple is now husband and wife
- Kiss
- Recessional

The Processional

Here comes the bride! That is, after her wedding party makes its way down the aisle first. As you and the other maids are waiting in the wings, ready to kick off the ceremony, think back to what you rehearsed: hold the bouquet loosely in front of you with both hands, stay calm and focused, walk in a leisurely pace (pausing briefly after each step), look straight ahead—and smile.

Certain religions offer slight variations on the order of the processional and recessional, and secular weddings usually borrow from these traditions. In general, at the start of a Christian or Roman Catholic ceremony, the groom and his best man will be waiting at the altar with the pastor or priest while the remaining groomsmen walk in from the church's side entrances in height order. In a Jewish ceremony, the procession includes the rabbi, the cantor (the person who leads the congregation in prayer), and both sets

"I had six bridesmaids and each one played her own special role. One was the peacemaker, one looked after me in her motherly way, one watched my hair and makeup with an eagle eye, one brought the party, and one just welled up with tears every time our eyes met. But I was most thankful for my matron of honor, Emily, who held my hair back in the catering closet as I barfed in a very un-bridal manner."—Katie of parents and grandparents. Here's a breakdown of the processional order for both Christian and Jewish ceremonies.

Christian or Roman Catholic
- Bridesmaids (starting with the attendant who will stand farthest from the bride and/or in height order with the shortest woman entering first)
- Junior bridesmaid(s)
- Maid or matron of honor
- Ring bearer (either alone or with the flower girl)
- Flower girl
- Bride, escorted by her father or another relative

Jewish
- Rabbi (leads the procession or awaits the others at the chuppah)
- Cantor
- Bride's grandparents
- Groom's grandparents
- Groom, escorted by his parents
- Bridesmaids (starting with the attendant who will stand farthest from the bride under the chuppah)
- Maid or matron of honor

- Ring bearer (either alone or with the flower girl)
- Flower girl
- Bride, escorted by her parents

At the Altar

When you proceed down the aisle, you and the other fe-male attendants will take your places beside the bride, to the left of the altar, in your designated order—typically by height, with the shortest bridesmaid standing farthest from the bride. If you're the honor attendant, you'll stand closest to the bride to signify your special role. Your posi-tion also makes it easy for you to hold the bride's bouquet as the couple prepares for the vow exchange and to hand the groom's ring to the officiant when they're ready to ex-change rings. Remember that photos will be snapped and video cameras will be rolling during the ceremony, so stand up straight, hold your bouquet with both hands at your natural waist, and be attentive. If you well up during the ceremony, it's okay. You probably won't be the only one in the room crying happy tears. If you typically get emotional at occasions like these, carry a pretty handkerchief with you so you can dab your eyes if and when you need to.

The Recessional

After the bride and groom are pronounced husband and wife, they will be the first to exit the church, followed by the wedding party and their parents. The recessional will be in the reverse order of the processional, with male attendants escorting the women.

Christian or Roman Catholic

- Bride and groom
- Flower girl and ring bearer
- Honor attendants (maid or matron of honor and best man)
- Junior bridesmaid(s)
- Bridesmaids and groomsmen, in pairs
- Parents of the bride (after the wedding party has exited)
- Parents of the groom
- Congregation

Jewish

- Bride and groom
- Bride's parents
- Groom's parents
- Bride's grandparents

- Groom's grandparents
- Flower girl and ring bearer
- Honor attendants (maid or matron of honor and best man)
- Bridesmaids and groomsmen, in pairs
- Rabbi and cantor

The next step in the proceedings depends on the day's schedule. If there will be photos taken at the church, the group could walk out the front door and then circle back around and reenter through a rear door. If the couple plans to have a receiving line at the ceremony site, you could just wait outside the door and greet guests as they leave the church.

The Receiving Line

Weddings attended by fifty people or more should have a receiving line—after all, this may be the couple's only chance to interact one-on-one with each of their guests. The line may form immediately following the ceremony or as guests arrive at the reception site. The bridal party isn't always invited to greet guests in the receiving line, but if you are asked to do so you should know what to expect.

As you stand in the line, take just a few seconds to shake hands with guests you don't know, briefly greet and hug those you do, and thank everyone for coming to the wedding (remember, you and the rest of the bridal party are honorary hosts of the festivities).

As part of your bridesmaid duties, you should also help to keep the line moving. If the bride's Great Aunt Margaret engages you in lengthy chatter, graciously end the conversation by telling her that you will catch up with her at the reception. Or if the bride and groom get tied up with a too-chatty guest, respectfully interrupt the conversation by introducing them to the next person in line.

THE RECEPTION

The formalities and pressures of the ceremony are over, the bride and groom are ecstatic now that they're finally husband and wife, friends and relatives are beaming—it's time to celebrate. But first there's the matter of getting to the reception site. The wedding party, including the bride and groom, may ride together in a large town car or stretch limo, and the photographer may also tag along to take a

"I had seven bridesmaids, two of whom were maids of honor. On my big day, they did everything to keep me calm and collected, even when things didn't go precisely according to plan. Your good friends will tell you the truth, but your best friends will tell little white lies if they know it's the right thing to do. —Abby few paparazzi-style candid shots. On the way over, get the party started by popping open a bottle of champagne and making the first toast to the newlyweds.

The reception typically kicks off with a cocktail hour, which may last a full hour or an hour and a half. This is your first opportunity to mingle at length with guests and make any necessary introductions. Next, you can expect the couple's grand entrance, their first dance, and the first course of the meal. The rest of the night will be sprinkled with toasts and speeches, more dancing, more mingling, and all-out revelry. The cake-cutting is usually done during the final hour of the reception, as the party is winding down. Before the couple's big send-off, the bride's honor attendant (and/or the other bridesmaids) should help her change into her going-away outfit, if she has one, and ensure that the honeymoon luggage is ready to go. It's the groomsmen's job to rig the getaway vehicle with "Just Married" signs, decals, and streamers—but you can clue them in as to the best time to accomplish their sneaky mission.

Dinner and Dancing

At the reception, the bridal party may be seated with the couple at a long head table or at a designated wedding-party table with their dates. If there's a head table, the bride and groom usually sit in the center facing the other tables, with the maid of honor seated next to the groom and the best man next to the bride; the attendants follow the same male-female pattern along the table. Another option is for all the bridesmaids to be seated on the bride's side of the table and all the groomsmen to be on the groom's side. The child attendants will be seated with their parents rather than at the head table.

After dinner is the best time for the wedding party to make their way to the dance floor, and they should encourage other guests to join in. Sometimes there's a fun song picked out for the bridesmaids to dance to. This can be a great ice breaker and a sure-fire way to energize the crowd. As the party goes on, feel free to let loose but remember that you still need to make a good impression. You're representing the bride, after all. Don't do anything embarrassing like getting sloppy drunk or dirty dancing with the groom's cute cousin. You can maintain your composure and still have a fabulous time.

Speeches and Toasts

If you're the honor attendant (or even if you're not), the reception is the place to give a well-thought-out speech to toast the bride and groom. The maid of honor's speech usually follows the best man's (typically after cocktails, before the meal has been served), but she shouldn't feel the need to top his groom-roasting musings. The other attendants might immediately follow with their own toasts or these may be interspersed throughout the meal, depending on how the toastmaster has scheduled them. If being witty is your usual personality, then by all means go for a laugh-inducing speech. But if that's not your style, then just speak from the heart. Focus on the strong bond you share with the bride, recount a funny anecdote about the couple's first date, or describe the moment she realized the groom was "the one." You could also borrow some words of inspiration from female writers, poets, philosophers, and celebrities. Whatever you do, go easy on the alcohol—at least until after your speech! Not big on public speaking? Keep the following tips in mind.

BE PREPARED. Practice your speech before the wedding to make sure you're comfortable speaking the words you've written—and that you're not rambling. It's also good to get feedback from at least one person. If you wrote your speech on note cards, have them at the ready. That way, you won't be fumbling for them when the toastmaster calls you up to the podium. Also be sure to have a glass of champagne (or another sparkling beverage if you don't drink) within arm's reach so you can make your toast at the end of the speech.

START WITH INTRODUCTIONS. Not everyone will know who you are, so state you name and your relationship to the bride and groom. Be specific about how and when you met the couple and perhaps how your friendship blossomed.

GIVE A TRIBUTE. This is the part of the speech when you'll share sweet anecdotes and thoughtful sentiments about the newlyweds. You can also include a quote, a short passage, or a song lyric in your tribute.

KEEP IT SHORT AND SWEET. Speeches should last no longer than three minutes. Remember to time yourself when practicing your speech so you have a sense of when you need to wrap things up.

CONCLUDE WITH YOUR TOAST. The official toast comes at the very end of your speech—it's when everyone in the room will follow your lead as you raise your glass to the couple. For example: "To Veronica and Charles! May the

··· MEMORABLE TOASTS ···

To make your toast especially poignant, meaningful, and memorable, begin with a passage about love or marriage, a sentiment you've heard from the bride or groom, or a traditional family toast if there is one (ask the parents of the couple). Here are some examples:

"Here's to health, peace, and prosperity; May the flower of love never be nipped by the frost of disappointment; nor the shadow of grief fall among a member of this circle." —Irish toast

"According to a Buddhist proverb, to say the words 'love and compassion' is easy, but to accept that love and compassion are built upon patience and perseverance is not easy. Rebecca and Tony, your marriage will be firm and lasting if you remember this. Cheers!"

"Laurie and Tom: In the words of Arlene Dahl, take each other for better or worse but not for granted. Here's to your marriage."

"Someone once said love is not finding someone to live with, it's finding someone you can't live without. Megan and Andrew, I wholeheartedly believe that you've both found that someone. Here's to your everlasting love."

joys you share today be only the beginning of a lifetime of love and happiness." For additional inspiration, see Memorable Toasts, page 137.

COUNTDOWN TO THE WEDDING

Need help keeping track of all your wedding-day to-dos? Here's a checklist to help keep you organized. Refer to this list often as you prepare for the big day, tweaking specific times and tasks as needed.

Eight-Plus Months Before
- Formally accept the bride's invitation to be part of the wedding party.
- Help the bride shop for her gown, the bridesmaid dresses, and accessories, if she'd like your input.
- Get professionally measured (bust, waist, hip, and dress length).

Five to Six Months Before
- Order your bridesmaid's dress. Check the receipt and confirm the following: style number, the size or measurements the salon is sending to the manufacturer, the

delivery date, the number of fittings included in the price, the amount of your deposit, and any remaining balance.

- Shop for your shoes and undergarments (a strapless bra or bustier, seamless underwear, and/or shapewear).

Two to Three Months Before
- Schedule your hair and makeup trials.
- Shop for your wedding gift.

Four to Six Weeks Before
- Formally RSVP for the wedding as soon as you receive the invitation, confirming whether you will be bringing a guest.
- Schedule your dress fittings (at least two). Make sure that you can move and sit comfortably in your gown.
- If you're the honor attendant or a willing bridesmaid, attend the bride's final dress fitting for a crash course on how to bustle her gown.

Two to Three Weeks Before
- Pick up your gown from the salon and try it on to make sure it fits properly.
- Get a facial.

- Get your hair trimmed and your final deep-conditioning hair treatment plus highlights or a gloss if you like.

One Week Before
- Get a body scrub.
- Attend the bridesmaid's luncheon, if it's held this week. It may also be held on the morning or afternoon of the wedding.
- Put together the bride's emergency kit.
- Practice your speech if you plan to make a toast at the reception.

One Day Before
- Attend the rehearsal and rehearsal dinner.
- Run any last-minute errands, per the bride's request.
- Get lots of sleep!

CH. 7

AFTER THE WEDDING

Thanks to the couple's long journey to the altar, the excitement of the wedding will linger on even after the last dance ends. Lucky for those who aren't quite ready to let the festivities end (including the newlyweds), there are plenty of opportunities for postwedding celebrations. It may start with a wedding after-party, which could be a preplanned affair or an impromptu late-night gathering at the hotel bar or bridal suite.

The morning after could be another opportunity to extend the party. These days, many couples stick around for a little while before riding off into the sunset—also known as the honeymoon—so they or their family might host a postwedding brunch as a final thank-you to guests, especially those who traveled a long distance to attend the wedding.

LET'S DO BRUNCH

These days, the postwedding brunch is typically hosted by the couple. However, the bride's parents may consider it an extension of their reception-hosting responsibilities and offer to pick up the tab. Or the groom's parents may choose to host. Regardless of who foots the bill, the brunch gives the newly-weds a chance to see and thank their guests once more before the honeymoon and to deliver a final farewell to guests who came from out of town. The guest list includes the couple's relatives and any other remaining wedding guests.

These events are especially common for weekend-long weddings or the ever-popular destination weddings. If the reception was held at a hotel or resort, the brunch (usually a buffet) will often take place in the main dining room or at one of the restaurants on site. Keep in mind it may be an early meal (perhaps no later than 11 A.M.) to accommodate check-out times. It might also be held at the home of the bride or groom's parents or at a favorite neighborhood diner. Unless you have a truly legitimate reason to miss the brunch, you and the other bridesmaids should make every effort to attend. Consider it your last official duty. Since the brunch is often informal,

"After the wedding, the bride took each of her bridesmaids out to lunch individually to thank them for their contribution to the wedding. We all appreciated the personal attention, and it really strengthened our friendship with her. I'll definitely do the same when I get married."

—Sarah

no speeches or toasts will be expected—but they certainly won't be discouraged.

POST-HONEYMOON WELCOME HOME

While the newlyweds are on their honeymoon, there are many gracious little things the wedding party can do to let them know they're still being thought of and wished the best. Ask around to find out when they're expected back, and display "Welcome Home" messages for them to see upon their return. Attach a sign to their mailbox or front door; if you were given the house keys, drape a banner from the walls of their foyer or leave a housewarming basket of fruit and other treats on their kitchen counter. You could also surprise the couple by having the ketubah (Jewish marriage license) framed for them. Or, if the attendants snapped candid photos throughout the wedding, upload the pictures onto a photo-sharing website and e-mail the link to the couple, their close friends, and family members. Seeing those photos will be a blast for the post-honeymoon newlyweds. Don't forget to enlist the groomsmen to help with these tasks.

IT'S A REUNION!

One way to cement the bond that you and the other brides-maids have formed is to check in with the bride and schedule at least one postwedding get-together immediately after the wedding. Go out for drinks after work one day, meet for lunch at an intimate café, or have a low-key dinner party at someone's home. It's a chance to reminisce about your favorite wedding moments, put the kibosh on any lingering tensions, and laugh off all the things that didn't quite go as planned—hey, they only make the day's memories more colorful. And if you develop a strong connection with the other attendants, consider arranging regular meet-ups.

Making Memories

If you and the other bridesmaids collected mementos (like a sample invitation, menu card, or program) while the bride was in full wedding-planning mode, use the time when the couple is away on their honeymoon to put together a personalized gift for them. Create a special wedding album, a whimsical scrapbook, or a shadow box filled with three-dimensional items such as dried flowers from the bridal bouquet, dress swatches, or inedible crystals and beads from the wedding cake.

You can present the finished keepsake to the bride during the postwedding bridesmaid get-together (in this case, the groom, as co-recipient, should also be invited) or save the gift for the couple's first wedding anniversary. Remember—your bridesmaid duties may end after the wedding, but your friendship duties will last a lifetime.

Appendix

BRIDESMAIDS' GOWNS & ACCESSORIES

DAVID'S BRIDAL
The retail bridal store has a large inventory of color-coordinated looks for the wedding party. The bride can check out the nifty Dress Your Wedding online tool to see how her attendants will look in the gowns and accessories she chooses.

www.davidsbridal.com
877-923-2749

J.CREW
The retailer's wedding collection includes affordable bridesmaids' dresses in a range of silhouettes and fabrics as well as a selection of shoes and accessories. Brides can contact a wedding specialist to help outfit their bridal party.

www.jcrew.com
800-562-0258

NICOLE MILLER
Each of the designer's bridesmaids' gowns is available in a wide range of colors. The latest styles can be found online.

www.nicolemiller.com
888-300-6258

PIPERLIME.COM
Gap's footwear offshoot features a selection of designer shoes appropriate for casual and black-tie weddings. The Web site offers free shipping and free returns on all Piperlime items.

www.piperlime.com
877-747-3754

PRONOVIAS

This Barcelona-based firm has long been known for making and distributing exquisite bridesmaids' dresses by top designers.

www.pronovias.com

SPANX

The company famous for its shapewear has seamless bras and panties, thigh smoothers, and tummy slimmers (including a maternity shaper) to keep you looking your best.

www.spanx.com
888-806-7311

THREAD BRIDESMAID

The New York–based company offers a huge selection of chic bridesmaids' dresses, including options for pregnant bridesmaids and junior bridesmaids. Orders and swatch requests can be placed online.

www.bridal.threaddesign.com
212-414-8844

VERA WANG

The luxury fashion brand best-known for its stylishly modern wedding gowns has a Maids line. Brides can go online to search for dresses by length, color, and fabric; contact a consultant; and e-mail their selections to their bridesmaids.

www.verawangonweddings.com
877-933-8372

ZAPPOS.COM

Brides can browse through more than 500 shoes in the bridesmaids' category alone, plus find accessories for the female attendants to match. Bonus: Free delivery for standard shipping and a one-year return policy.

www.zappos.com
800-927-7671

HAIR & MAKEUP

ELIZABETH ARDEN RED DOOR SPAS

With more than two dozen day spa and resort locations nationwide, Red Door Spas offer a diverse menu of beauty services, including makeup trials and bridal half- and full-day spa packages.

www.reddoorspas.com

BOBBI BROWN COSMETICS

Schedule personalized makeup sessions covering bridal beauty basics at the flagship studio in New York, or get answers to your beauty questions via live chats with makeup artists.

www.bobbibrowncosmetics.com
877-310-9222

LIPS & LOCKS

This L.A. studio, headed by hair and makeup artist Sheree Pouls, whose experience ranges from special events and runway shows to TV and feature films, offers bridal styling and consultations as well as makeup lessons.

www.lipsandlocks.com
310-301-8086

ONCE UPON A BRIDE SALON

This New York–based salon, helmed by celebrity stylist Stacey Lyn Weinstein, specializes in wedding services and offers makeup air-brushing and eyelash extensions.

www.ouab.com
212-353-2350

SEPHORA

Step into your nearest store for a complimentary wedding-day makeup consultation and free product samples. Reservations are recommended.

www.sephora.com
877-737-4672

DAY SPAS & TANNING SALONS

Bliss Spas

A visit to one of this company's many locations will have you blissed out and beautiful for the big day.

www.blissworld.com

mobileSPA

If you're planning a bachelorette spa party, this company will send beauty specialists to your home for facials, manicures, pedicures, and massages. Bridal packages are also on offer.

www.mobilespa.com
800-651-4740

SPARTY!

The company arranges custom or à la carte spa parties, complete with cocktails and a personalized menu, for bridal showers, bachelorette parties, or wedding-day pampering at your home or its New York loft.

www.spa-party.com
646-736-1777

St. Tropez Tanning

Check the Web site to find a list of spas that offer this brand's services and spray tanning booths or to purchase sunless-tanning products for at-home applications.

www.sttropeztan.com
800-366-6383

THE BRIDESMAID'S COMPANION

PARTY SUPPLIES

CRANE & CO

Crane's is an option for eco-conscious party planners. The company has an entirely "green" selection of fine stationery made from 100 percent recovered cotton fibers and uses only water-based inks or those made with naturally renewable vegetable oils.

www.crane.com
800-268-2281

KATE'S PAPERIE

The online or bricks-and-mortar stores in New York are a quality resource for elegant custom, printable, and fill-in bridal shower invitations.

www.katespaperie.com
800-809-9880

LEE'S ART SHOP, INC.

Billed as "The Department Store for the Artist," this shop offers a unique assortment of supplies and inspiration for party decorations and keepsakes.

www.leesartshop.com
212-247-0110

MICHAELS

Here's a one-stop shop for all your DIY-project needs—including scrap-booking supplies and memory books as well as party decorations, favors and props.

www.michaels.com
800-642-4235

INDEX

Acknowledgments

To my sister, for whom I was truly honored to be maid of honor—and to my parents who have always showered me with unconditional love and support.

Thanks also go to David Tutera and Stacey Lyn Weinstein for their contributions, Amy Elliott for her faith in me, and all the fantastic people I worked with at Hearst Books. Finally, thank you to all the generous brides and bridesmaids who took the time to share their cherished memories and pearls of wisdom.